Guiding
Diverse Flocks

TALES OF A RURAL MENNONITE PASTOR

ERNIE HILDEBRAND

To Irene, Art has been a great salesman, distributing this book! Trust you enjoy reading it. I never expected to write this book, but here it is!

Ernie.

 FriesenPress

One Printers Way
Altona, MB R0G 0B0
Canada

www.friesenpress.com

Copyright © 2021 by Ernie Hildebrand
First Edition — 2021

All rights reserved.

No part of this publication may be reproduced in any form, or by any means, electronic or mechanical, including photocopying, recording, or any information browsing, storage, or retrieval system, without permission in writing from FriesenPress.

ISBN
978-1-03-912031-0 (Hardcover)
978-1-03-912030-3 (Paperback)
978-1-03-912032-7 (eBook)

1. BIOGRAPHY & AUTOBIOGRAPHY, RELIGIOUS

Distributed to the trade by The Ingram Book Company

"I do it (write my story) because it seems to me that no matter who you are, and no matter how eloquent or otherwise, if you tell your story with sufficient candor and concreteness, it will be an interesting story and in some sense a universal story. I do it also in the hope of encouraging others to do the same."

—Frederick Buechner (theologian, author)

"One of the tasks of being an elderly person, is to dig through the compost dump of your life and to sift through all your various memories—the people you met, the places you have been and to organize them in such a way that you can hold unto what was most meaningful."

—John H. Neufeld (President at CMBC 1984–97)

TABLE OF CONTENTS

Forward	ix
Earliest Memories	1
Life Growing Up On The Farm	5
Farming, Married with Children	17
Major Decision Time	29
West to Osler, Saskatchewan	39
From Osler to Swift Current	51
Back to Manitoba, Springstein	67
Major Decision Two	81
Coming Full Circle, Home	87
Life as a Student	103
Life as a Carpenter	115
Life as a Shepherd	131
Life as a Protester	143
Journey of Faith	151
Life in Retirement	161
Afterword	181
Tribute to Linda	185
Guatemalan Guest is now Springstein's "Disappeared"	187
A January Morning on the Farm	191
Hildebrand Reunion 2008	195
+55 Canada Games	199

Forward

It is November 26, 2020. The coronavirus (Covid-19) has been with us since March of this year, when almost everything was shut down. After a brief respite over the summer, when some style of socializing was permitted, the virus came back with a vengeance in early November. Curling was cancelled on November 6. Since that has been my main winter activity for several years, I wondered how I would get through the winter months.

Over the years, it has been suggested to me several times by different people that I should write details about my journey. I have avoided this suggestion, but it was something to consider, and I mulled over how I might eventually tackle this project, if I did at all. On Monday, November 23, 2020, I decided, rather abruptly, to begin. I approached the keyboard and started on my earliest memories. That went OK. My next thought was to write about my carpentry ventures. By now I had a format in mind. I wasn't going to take a strictly chronological approach but would identify stories that covered most of my life. As I think ahead, the next one might be titled, "Our Two Best Decisions." Later on, these stories will need to be arranged in some order. We'll see how it goes.

The virus will be with us for some time. Vaccines are being developed, which is our best hope of getting rid of it. Best estimates are that the vaccines might be available to us by spring or early summer 2021. So I have a lot of time. In a little more than a week, I'll be turning seventy-eight. Finishing the book before I'm eighty will be an objective—that is, printed and delivered!

I have a copy of Dad's (Jacob Hildebrand) book, *A Backward Glance*, that I refer to for some details, such as what kind of car we had when Linda came home after her birth in 1947. Dad was a remarkable storyteller and writer. I won't attempt to match him, but I won't let that intimidate me either. I have a great deal more formal education than he had—he only had Grade Eight. But education doesn't make up for natural gifts and his determination to master the English language! I think of myself as a pretty good storyteller, but one less capable of putting these stories down on paper. Judy, my wife of fifty-five years, has served as editor for me in the past. She might have a big job ahead of her. I am somewhat hopeful that my style will be preserved ... after all, Rudy Wiebe, celebrated Canadian author, writes in many incomplete sentences!

To help potential readers who are not familiar with our life, I offer a brief outline.

> 1942–1965: I lived on my parents' farm, south of Crystal City, Manitoba.
>
> 1965–1971: I moved half-a-mile south to the farm purchased from the Stewarts. I was married to Judy, and our first three children were born during these years.
>
> 1971–1974: I Studied at Canadian Mennonite Bible College (now CMU) in Winnipeg. We came back to the farm for one last crop in 1972.
>
> 1974–1980: We moved to Osler, Saskatchewan. I took a position as pastor in the church there. Our fourth child was born in 1975.
>
> 1980–1990: We moved to Swift Current, Saskatchewan. I took a faculty position with Swift Current Bible Institute for six years. I also worked with Cypress Hills Community College in adult education and with the Neil Squire Foundation for four years.
>
> 1990–1994: We moved back to Manitoba to Springstein, where I pastored Springstein Mennonite Church.

Forward

1994–2002: We moved back to our farm at Crystal City, and I accepted a part-time position as pastor at Trinity Mennonite Fellowship, Mather, Manitoba. I became a bi-vocational pastor and shepherd.

2002—2015: I entered semi-retirement, having completed eight years at TMF. I concentrated on our sheep farm and continuing our Poplarlane B&B.

2015: We established a new yard on a sub-divided portion of our farm. We had sold the rest of the home quarter, and we entered a new phase of retirement. This is the third location along Cypress Creek on which I have lived.

Some explanations are required. Our family has always associated with what was called the General Conference Mennonite Church. A name change took place in 2000, and it's now called Mennonite Church Canada. We're a national grouping of congregations. There are many different Mennonite groupings. Some refer to these groupings as different denominations of Mennonites, but I prefer to see all Mennonites as one denomination organized into a variety of conferences. Our conference would be considered the most "liberal" of all the groups. Divorce is now allowed. We have female pastors in many congregations. Other world religions are respected. Sexual orientation has been thoroughly debated, and several congregations call themselves "welcoming churches." The first gay wedding in one of our congregations has been conducted. This last issue has caused a lot of dissension, and many congregations have chosen to leave the conference. These issues haven't been addressed by the more conservative Mennonite conferences. There is considerable variation in approaches to belief and practice in these conferences as well.

Both of my parents were born in Southern Russia just before the beginning of World War One and the Russian Revolution. Stories of that period have been well documented. Both of their families came to Canada in the 1920s and settled in Manitoba. When my parents married in 1939 and began farming at Crystal City, we were a Mennonite, German-speaking family who stuck fairly closely to the small group of Mennonite families in the area. Gradually, English became the predominant language in our household, spurred on by us kids entering the public school in town. At that time, the pressure was on uniformity in society. Immigrants were expected to integrate into the existing culture, and our families did that to a large extent. Today there is more respect for diversity, which can make all lives richer. Families and different cultural/religious groups have chosen different routes. The paths the Mennonite people chose vary a great deal. I respect people for their choices, as I trust others will respect ours.

Earliest Memories

Having experienced close to eighty years since my entrance into this world, it's time to document some of this journey. I'm fascinated with the age of one's first memories. I asked my eleven-year-old granddaughter if she could remember feeding the sheep on our farm six years ago: "Not really," she replied. How about playing on the bales stored under the shelter? This elicits an affirmative response. She didn't have the patience to explore this further. However, trying to determine one's earliest memory is interesting. Four of our grandchildren had a great time playing on our sheep farm. Much time was spent out there while doing chores, especially during lambing time. Kathryn was heard singing at the top of her lungs while spreading out alfalfa hay for the lambs: "Keep on the sunny side, always on the money side! Keep on the sunny side of life!" Then there were the horses. Susanna enjoyed buckboard rides. At one-and-a-half-years of age, she would bounce up and down and say "Papa" and then snort like a horse. Her signal to me. How could I turn her down? I want them to remember those times.

So what do I remember? My first home was a fourteen-by-sixteen-foot dwelling. When I consider that the barn I built on our new acreage in 2015 is sixteen-by-twenty, I can scarcely believe it. (Later, an eight-by-fourteen-foot addition was added.) Mom, Dad, Elfrieda, and I were the occupants here in December 1942, after I joined the family. When Linda joined our family in March 1947, our number increased to five. I remember teasing Linda that she insisted right away that Dad would need to upgrade the house, for it was inadequate for her taste! This did happen. Dad dug a basement that spring, and construction began on a modern one-and-a-half-storey house.

I don't remember much about that first dwelling, other than watching it being moved off our yard to a farm one mile west. What I do remember is being put to bed in my crib. When I'd look straight up from my pillow, I'd see the wall-mounted big box of a telephone right over my head. I feared that it might become unfastened from the wall and crash on my head. This will have to serve as my earliest fear. Not sure at what age I left the crib ... maybe not until Linda was born,

which would make me four-and-a-half years old.

I do have several memories of March 1947. While Mom was in the hospital giving birth to Linda, Elfrieda and I stayed with Uncle Abe and Aunt Mary Klassen on their farm. It was spring with melting snow and puddles. Elfrieda reminded me of the following story recently. We were running on planks to the outdoor biffy west of their house. The running caused splashing, and our Sunday church clothes were dirtied. Aunt Mary was not impressed, so both of us got a licking. It was likely this that caused me to tell my aunt that now I knew why she had no children of her own—"Because you don't like children!" (I would have said this in German.)

During that same stay, I remember going to Pilot Mound with Uncle Abe on some business he needed to conduct. Walking past a hardware store, I stopped to admire a large yellow construction toy in the window. I told Uncle Abe, again in German, "You can easily afford to buy that for me!" And he did! I must have been a too smart-alecky kid to have around. Or maybe I was considered cute at that age. A narrow difference at times!

The time arrived for our departure, as Linda was coming home. Dad must have picked us up first and then travelled to Crystal City to pick up Mom and Linda. The last two miles west of Highway 17 (later changed to 34) on the way home were not much more than a dirt trail. At places it got very slippery with a danger of getting stuck. To avoid these spots, Dad would turn into the ditch which was grassed and therefore firm (so the road must have been graded). Once past the bad spot, he'd drive back on the road. Mom was not impressed, I remember. Linda didn't comment! Recently, I've tried to recall the type of car that must have been, but I draw a blank. It was likely some kind of Ford with a back seat. Model Ts were built until 1927. The model A followed until 1931 and then the B, 1931–34. Dad's first car was a 1929 model A that he purchased in 1936. Not sure if he still had that car in 1947, but I suspect he upgraded along the way. I recall it as a four-door with the back doors opening outward from the front, not the back. This style was built in the 1940s. The first new car I remember was the 1951 brand-new Ford. It was likely purchased that year as well.

Mulling over transportation, I remember Mom coming home from town once with a one-horse buggy after going grocery shopping. The groceries were stored behind the seat. I recall admiring the horse and the buggy with springs, which made for a smoother ride. It wasn't ours. We didn't have a horse like that or a buggy. I can only speculate that it might have been Uncle Henry's, a younger brother of Mom's, who might have come from Snowflake to help on the farm for a few days. Horses were still a major way of travel, especially in winter, when cars were parked. I was reminded of this recently when I saw an early picture of the Mennonite church built in 1948. While not in the picture, a barn was also built just northwest of the church. I believe it held about a dozen teams, maybe twenty.

Ernie with his mother and sister, Elfrieda, ca. 1944

The main transportation in winter was by horse and sleigh. We only ever had an open sleigh, and I envied those families who had closed cabooses with a small wood burning stove. What luxury! Dad finally bought one of those at a farm auction, but I don't remember using it. It was too late. It was obsolete, so it was parked in the barnyard. Cars became our year-round transportation when better roads were built. I think I was beginning to understand that we were "poor cousins." Most of Dad's brothers drove better cars, like Buicks and Oldsmobiles, and Chryslers. The Harms drove Dodges purchased at Voth's in Manitou. We drove Fords. We got our first Dodge in 1957, but by then it wasn't much of a car. The '57 Dodge must be one of the ugliest cars ever built! Hold on, I must be in my teenage years–well beyond earliest memories!

Back to earlier memories. Our first barn was a bank barn built into the creek bank. It would have had a loft at some time. Dad had placed a flat roof on it made with tree trunks and then covered with straw. This served the purpose for a while. In 1943–44, a new round-roof barn was constructed with a big loft.

I would have been around two years old. This might be earlier than the threat of the telephone! I remember pigs being kept in the old barn for several more years. The new barn had a lean-to on the north side. The roof was finished, except for the shingles. I recall climbing up a ladder and crawling onto the roof, which was gently sloped—a great place to run around and a new view from being at ground level. I wasn't afraid of heights and was tolerated up there. I don't recall any adults telling me to get off the roof. The main part of the barn was still under construction, for I remember hearing hammers busy at work. The barn still stands today! Ray Tiessen, my nephew, is dedicated to preserving the barn. The lean-to has been removed, but the new red steel siding and the black steel roof makes it a great sight on what is now #3 Highway, also a vast improvement over the dirt road we travelled years ago.

So much for early memories. Sorry, David, I don't have details of your arrival in 1948. I would have been six by then, but my companion was Elfrieda, two years older than me. A baby brother wasn't much of a playmate.

Life Growing Up
On The Farm

I grew up on the farm in the 1940s and 1950s. The world and the farm were both very different from what they are today. I believe the 1950s was a transition decade, from farming with horses to farming with modern agricultural equipment. However, life at that time seemed normal and much better than the previous decade of drought and depression. The farm was a carefree place to grow up. We had a creek to explore right next to the yard. I'd gather the planks and pillars, which were the remains of bridges destroyed by the spring floods, and use them to build a raft. They got a lot of use, sailing from the yard to the bridge north of the yard and back. My brother, Davie, and our dog would be the crew. My parents had little idea of what we were doing. "Out playing," they assumed. We didn't know how to swim and there were no life jackets. We were careful and fell off only on occasion, but thankfully in more shallow areas. We knew where the deep parts were, for we used long poles to propel the raft. I learned that the raft needed to be pulled up a bit out of the water when we were finished sailing for the day. When I hadn't done this and had left the raft for some time, it got waterlogged and didn't support our weight when we launched it. That time we took a spill! One spring a large bridge pillar washed up in our pasture. It was about eight feet long and two feet in diameter. I was determined to hollow it out with a hammer and chisel to fashion a canoe! I spent many hours at this project. I never made much progress and eventually left it. Years later, I'd see this pillar and my determined efforts to fulfill a dream! I was reminded of this childhood project whenever I observed our own children, and later grandchildren, work with frustration on projects beyond their capability. Imaginations working overtime, but that's childhood.

David with dog and Ernie ca. 1953

As a boy, I was fascinated with tractors. I'm told that at two or three years of age, I climbed up onto the seat of a John Deere row crop tractor. The engine was running, and I pushed forward on the hand clutch. Thankfully, the tractor was in low gear and the front wheels were turned, so I drove in circles until someone spotted me! Next, Dad purchased a Massey Harris 30 and later a Co-op E3. Somewhere along the line, he also bought a Fordson Major, which was the worst choice ever. It was difficult to start and very heavy in the front, so it often got stuck when the front tires got mired in a wet spot on the field. (Normally it was the big, rear drive wheels that would get a tractor stuck.) These tractors were all in the thirty horsepower range.

During these years, we still had one or two teams of horses that were used for chores, but more importantly during haying and harvest. Harvest has always been the most exciting time for me. I recall driving the tractor while pulling a binder. The binder would cut the grain and tie it into sheaves. The sheaves, after they were tied, would end up on a bundle carrier, which would deposit them when five had been collected. Dad would ride on a seat on the binder manipulating all the levers and press the trip to dump the sheaves in uniform rows. These binders had earlier been pulled by horses; it was a one-man operation. It must have been a very skilled person to manipulate all the levers as well as to guide the four-horse team pulling the binder. Horses were well trained, however, and would readily turn the corners, etc.

Now a kid was required to operate the tractor. I was likely eight or nine years of age. I'd get sleepy, and the tractor would move out of line too far from where the binder was to cut the standing grain. Dad would shout to wake me up! I don't remember doing much of this. Later, when a combine was purchased, the binder was converted to lay down a swath instead of creating sheaves. This machine was used to cut the grain until Dad could afford to buy a swather. But it was the threshing machine that really created the excitement! It would be set up on a field close to the yard. Teams of horses pulling racks would gather the sheaves from the field (the sheaves had been set up in stooks to shed the rain) and bring them to the threshing machine, where they'd be forked in by hand. Straw would be blown out the back to create a big pile after a day's harvest, and the separated grain would end up in a wagon box to be hauled by horses to a granary.

I would often accompany Vin McGill, whose job it was to haul the grain. He was a jovial neighbour who told great stories and smoked a pipe. He would transfer the grain into the granary with a grain scoop, as there were no augers. I was likely always in the way of his work, but don't recall any reprimand. It was the McGill family who made salmon sandwiches to be shared by harvest crews! I really enjoyed this taste. We never had them at home. I would also go along with another crew that gathered up the sheaves. I'd ride on the load and try to help arrange the sheaves on the rack. I wanted to fork them into the machine but was likely getting in the way. I was determined that by the next harvest season, I would be strong enough to handle my own team, but that would never happen. Dad bought a small combine and sold the threshing machine! The big crews of men gathering to help each other out to harvest their crops came to an end. The crews had been made up of neighbours and some hired help. The harvest machinery and crew would move around the neighbourhood as each had a crop to harvest. There must have been fifteen to twenty men involved, and the women fed them all! My mom, in her retirement home, wondered why Dad wouldn't hire help for her to feed the crew, since he hired men to help him!

I experienced boyhood on the farm with little distinction between play and work. Both were exciting, and I longed to get more involved as I grew bigger and stronger. At play, Davie and I designed elaborate miniature farmsteads under the trees close to the house. We would bring out farm toys and set up fields and pastures. I would buy a roll of stovepipe wire at the hardware store in town and use it to build fences equipped with gates. This wire was very thin and easily bent into the required shape. I had watched and helped Dad with the many fences on the farm, so I had full knowledge of how fences were built. Livestock was the major income source on the badly-eroded farm that he had bought. The acres seeded to grain crops were limited.

Winters provided an entirely different experience on the prairies. Milk and beef cattle were housed in the barn and needed to be fed, and the barn needed to be cleaned out on a daily basis. This wasn't as enjoyable as the summer activities. Thankfully, Dad never asked us kids to help with morning chores before we boarded the school bus. Some of my cousins weren't that fortunate. Evening chores, however, required our help. We had a big pond on the creek just down the hill from our yard. In winter, this was a good area for skating. I'd head down the hill after school with a shovel to clean the snow off the ice. Before I could strap on my skates, I'd get the call to come up to start the chores! When I was older, I noted that I'd become experienced in shovelling snow but never learned to skate! The quality of our skates was also an issue.

Saturdays were different. One Saturday, Elfrieda, Linda, and I were down on the creek. We had cleaned off the snow and were finally skating when we became aware of a figure standing on the high bank on the far side of the creek looking down on our activity. He was dressed for the weather and carrying some supplies. He stood for a while and then moved further on and out of sight. We weren't necessarily afraid, but we were troubled. We related this experience to our parents later over supper. Dad said that the man was a trapper from Swan Lake. His people had occupied this land decades ago, and we shouldn't fear him. He would cause us no harm. Later, in recalling this incident, I thought that he had likely approached us while walking on the ice. He didn't want to startle us, so he moved up on the bank to get by us. Once he was by us, he'd return to continue on his trapline at ice level. He was far from his home on the reservation, so he would have been equipped to spend several nights outside. Swan Lake is fifty kilometres. from our farm by road. That was my first encounter with an Indigenous person.

Harvesting was about to change. In 1951, Dad purchased a small combine and sold the threshing machine. The combine was a Dearborn Wood Bros. machine. It came equipped with a gas engine and could easily be pulled by the Co-op E3 tractor. The grain tank could hold twenty-five bushels of wheat. It was built by a small company in the USA that never became popular like John Deere or Massey Harris, but it was likely the cheapest option at the time. The farm was cash poor. During the first two years, a neighbour did the trucking of the grain. In return, Dad combined the neighbour's crop. I don't think we had more than one hundred acres in crop at the time.

For the 1953 crop, Elfrieda and I convinced Dad that we could handle the trucking. We had an old truck we could drive and an auger by that time. We needed to back up to the auger, start the auger motor by pulling a rope, and then shovel the grain out through a hole in the back. Then we'd go back to the field. Finally, I wasn't just playing at harvest but, together with my sister, was a vital cog in the harvest crew. (A few years later, Dad bought a better truck, and still later added a hoist. The land base had grown, and a bigger and better combine was purchased.)'

Ernie, David, Linda, Elfrieda ca. 1950

The 1953 harvest was nearing completion. School would soon be starting, and the fun would be over. Who could have anticipated what was about to occur? Late one afternoon, I had come back to the field after leaving Elfrieda with the truck. I ran to catch up with the combine. The grain hopper was poorly designed, so I would climb up on the moving machine to the hopper to move the grain into the corners so the hopper could fill more fully. There was no ladder, but I had made this move all fall with no fear. But this time, I must have slipped. I fell in front of the tire. This was the combine's "big" tire, which was on the side of the engine and the full grain tank of wheat. The tire rolled over the right side of my head. I was in serious shape but never lost consciousness. I was aware of Dad running back to me and beckoning Elfrieda to come with the truck. They loaded me into the truck and then into the car on the yard and we were off to the local hospital in Crystal City. Mom was holding me in the back seat and praying. She told Dad to hurry and disregard the stop sign on the way to the hospital. Dad refused her wish, saying he didn't want to have another accident.

At the hospital, I was placed on a stretcher. At one point I was moved down some stairs, I think to take some X-rays. The decision was made to transfer me to the Morden hospital by ambulance. I remember going down the hill at La Riviere. I must have lost consciousness at times or simply slept. It was determined that there were no broken bones, and no surgery was required, but healing would take some time. At one point they contemplated extracting all my teeth, but this was never required. Mom came every day and stayed with me for ten days. Doctors and nurses cared for me, checking under the bandages and giving me a "shot" on my bum! I had no idea what my face looked like and begged Mom to let me take a look in a mirror. She refused. One day I convinced a nurse to move the dresser, which had a mirror, so I could see myself. She consented. I guess she told Mom what she had done and apologized. She said that I had taken one look, never said a word, and lay back down on my pillow. I was a dreadful sight. I got lots of get-well cards from cousins and school mates. One card stood out. It was from Judy. She and I had had a "fling" a few years earlier! Would she still love me if she saw how I now looked? I had considerable doubts.

A large family wedding was to take place during this time. Relatives would be travelling from the west to a Mennonite village east of Morden, where the wedding would take place. My cousins wanted to see me, and the plan was for them to stop by at the hospital after the wedding. I would come to the outside door, where they would gather. I was really excited about it, but I'm not sure what I envisioned. I think I hoped we would visit like we normally had. I was in for a shock! I was met by a sea of pained faces and utter silence. No one responded to my attempt at conversation. I was ushered back to my room deeply disappointed. The reality of my facial disfigurement was sinking in.

The recovery took some time. I had two corrective surgeries within the next six months but carried on at school in between hospital stays. I tried to adapt to these new circumstances, but I spent too much time looking in the mirror and worrying about the disfigurement. Over the next few years, there was considerable improvement. It did seem to bother me more than anyone else, and I don't recall negative comments.

I was getting older and able to do more of the work on the farm. I always considered field work with equipment enjoyable. Winter chores, milking cows, and cleaning out the barn with the horses were more of a drudgery. The horses needed to be harnessed, and I learned how to do it, but they were huge and the harnesses were heavy. We had a number of different teams of horses over the years. Dad had purchased a young team of "blacks" that had unlimited energy and were difficult to control. The stone boat used for hauling out the manure to spread on the winter fields had no front on it to help with balance. It was just a flat sled. I would take the load out to the field at top speed and begin to unload the manure. Once unloaded, the team would head back to the yard at full speed. A number of times, I lost my balance, and the team ran away on me. I was slender with not much weight, so I couldn't hold them back. The team would end up somewhere, caught in a fence or something, usually with some torn harness that Dad would have to repair. It was really a problem.

I decided to tire out the horses by forcing them to run with the full load and circle the twenty-acre field at full speed before unloading the manure. This didn't really affect them a great deal. I eventually was able to fashion a front to the stone boat, which gave me the support I needed and also a place to tie up the reins when we were stopped. Dad took this team to town one time when the roads were blocked and reported that they travelled at top speed both ways. We were six miles from town. Later, this team was replaced with the gentlest team, who would never start moving until one gave them an audible signal. A welcome relief!

The teams of horses weren't just used for farm chores. They were also our family transportation in the winter for several years. In my earlier years of going to school, we needed to go two miles east of our home to catch the school bus that would take us to town. We'd get a ride by car in the morning but usually walked the two miles home in the afternoon. One winter, we had a big snowstorm, so many roads were blocked with snow. That week, Dad hitched up the horses and took Elfrieda and me to catch the school bus. This interrupted his chore schedule, so he proposed that we kids take the team to the highway, turn it around to face back home, tie the reins up in a way to allow the team to trot, and send them on their way. We did that; however, when they got to the turn off to our yard, they went straight ahead, crossed the bridge, and continued on their way. Lucky for Dad, he saw what had happened and phoned the neighbours two miles to the west, asking them to stop the team and send them back our way. Dad went out to the road to intercept them this time. Then they were put to work doing the chores. They had already travelled eight miles, so Dad decided to place a strand of barb wire across the road to guide the team off the road and onto our yard. This worked perfectly for a few days, but then the snowplow came down the road and didn't see the wire. The plow broke the wire, which scratched our car, which was parked on the road due to our snow-blocked lane! A comedy of errors? I'm not sure who was laughing, other than the snowplow operator!

One winter on the last day of school before Christmas, there was no one to meet us when we got off the bus on our way home. It was bitterly cold with a northwest wind, and we were both chilled to the bone by the time we reached the nearest yard, half a mile from the highway. We didn't know the Stewart family very well, only Mr. Stewart himself. (No relation to Lorne Stewart). Elfrieda and I wondered what to do. We were too cold to continue, so we approached the house and knocked on the door. We were warmly invited to come in and get warmed up. The two women seemed delighted to have children stop for a visit! We got cookies and milk and warmed up rather quickly. When we said we would be on our way, they thought we should stay, for surely our parents would come and get us. But we persisted and started home. We made good time after having been warmed up properly. Dad wasn't home. He had intended to pick us up in town after school but got there too late, and the bus had left. I don't recall an apology! Our family didn't say "sorry' readily.

One fall day when I came home from school, the weather was great and I had some fantastic plans for the late afternoon and early evening. I came in the door, and Mom told me that Dad was expecting me out at the potato patch. He had been "lifting" spuds all afternoon, and it was up to Elfrieda and I to gather them in pails and then transfer them into sacks. My plans were sure shattered. My play plans gone. Dad always planted enough potatoes for our own use and then many more to sell through the local store. The grocer would then give Dad credit toward groceries. I sure wasn't going to do that when I was older!

There were also times to play. Some of my play involved my closest neighbour friend who lived two-and-a-half miles away. We would meet occasionally in the summer to swim in the dugout in our pasture ... well, neither of us could swim very well, but we used old tubes that would still hold air as floating devices. I also played a little hardball in town after school. My friend Clare was the pitcher. We never had a coach, and this fifteen-and-under team had no truly talented athletes. I played shortstop or third base but had difficulty throwing as far as first base, so an infield hit resulted in a safe hit for our opposition! I'm not sure if we ever won a game. I hit a double in one game and felt it was a major accomplishment. Meanwhile, our opposition was hitting home runs. I had bought a new "Black Diamond" glove (that I still have) and shoes with cleats for footwear. I was well equipped, but that didn't lead to success.

Clare also introduced me to professional football. He was a Winnipeg Blue Bombers fan and followed the games on the radio. He talked about all the different teams in western Canada and the competition the Bombers faced. I began to listen to the games as well. We had played some flag football at school, so I basically knew how the game was played. I was hooked. In November 1957, my brother and I walked south to the Stewart farm to watch the Grey Cup game on their TV. Lorne Stewart was also a football fan and welcomed us when I phoned to ask permission to come. Their TV reception was very poor. There was a lot of "snow" on the screen, but on occasion we did see parts of the game. It was also disappointing that the Bombers lost badly to Hamilton, but I was able to talk to Clare about the game the following week in school!

Later in life, I'd suggest that if we'd stayed home and "watched" the game on the radio, we would have seen almost as much! The next year, Davie and I walked north to the McGill neighbours. Their reception was much better, and the Bombers won in a thrilling game! By 1959 we had our own TV. We were the first Mennonite family in our area to purchase this largely feared and somewhat forbidden object!

I've been a CFL fan ever since, although I changed my allegiance to the Saskatchewan Roughriders. I had tired of Winnipeg sportswriters bad-mouthing the Riders and suggesting they should be banned from the league. I decided to cheer for these underdogs. Then we ended up living in that province for sixteen years! I've never missed watching the Grey Cup game since that first one at the Stewarts' house! This last year (2020), the game wasn't played due to the pandemic. I realize I'm getting carried away here, but I need to mention the arrangement we had while living at Osler years later. The Kruger family found out that I was a football fan and issued an annual invitation to our family to spend the Grey Cup afternoon with them so we could watch the game together. The Grey Cup was now being played on Sundays, and they noted that pastor families could get an invitation for Sunday dinner from a non-football family! This way, we could politely decline, saying we had a previous invitation. This worked out well!

Saturday evenings in summer during my boyhood were special events. The town businesses were open late in the evening, and the town was bustling, with the majority of farm families going to town for business at this time every week. We kids received a small allowance, and I would go to the Chinese restaurant and order a float. It was an Orange Crush drink poured over two scoops of ice cream! Other times, most of the evening was spent in the barber shop. We didn't make appointments, so we had our haircut in the order of appearance. There could be a dozen people ahead of one in line. We weren't to go into the pool room at the back of the barber shop, but often we did.

At that time on the farm there was no easy marker between being a kid and becoming an adult, and there was no young adult category. At twelve to fourteen years of age, we worked like an adult, and in some respects were treated as such. My experience growing up on the farm also proved true the saying, "You can take the boy out of the country, but you can't take the country out of the boy!"

Farming, Married with Children

In the spring of 1961, I was back on the farm full-time. I had completed the two-year agriculture course after opting out of high school. The university course was designed for students from the farm and ran from early October till early April. This accommodated harvest and spring seeding seasons, unlike high school. That was all behind me now. No more interruptions! I was prepared to farm with my dad for the next while and hopefully get a farm of my own eventually. Our land base had increased by this time. Dad had rented 600 acres of crop land that adjoined our farm. The total cropland had increased to 750 acres. About 560 acres would be seeded every year with the rest in summer fallow. Summer fallow was practised for weed control and moisture preservation. Our machinery had been upgraded as well, with two tractors in the fifty to fifty-five horsepower range and a newer pull-type combine. The livestock operation consisted of ten dairy cows, twenty-five to thirty beef cows, pigs, and some chickens and laying hens. My priority remained with the field crops. I didn't like the dairy cream shipping enterprise. As a recent agri-grad, I advocated for their sale. It was time to specialize, university profs had told us. But fathers were not easily persuaded by the "experts!"

I struck out on my own within this operation by adding a flock of sheep. Dad was supportive of this decision. By that fall, I had a flock and the necessary housing for this start.

I celebrated my nineteenth birthday in December and had for some time wondered how to start dating and looking for a lifelong mate. These two aspects were not separated in my mind. I hadn't considered recreational, casual dating. My date would need to be a prospective mate, at least. Of course, it would need to be agreed upon by both! But how to go about this? I was shy with girls and couldn't handle teasing by my family. I'd need to coordinate an activity, call a girl, and arrange to borrow the family car. This was a massive operation! Where does one start? Suitable activities were few in our rural community, and it couldn't be too public an event, like a hockey game. I chose a movie that was featured in the theatre in Pilot Mound. The film had an Australian setting and included a sheep station. This would give me something to talk about!

I decided to call Judy and invite her out for that evening. This was another complication, since it was frowned upon to date someone who already had a boyfriend. But how was I to know? I decided to take my chance, but I couldn't call from home, where the whole family would eavesdrop. The telephone was a wall mount, centrally located in the house, and offered no privacy. What if she turned me down? I would need to make sure the car was available and drive to town and call from the pay booth. It wouldn't be much notice for her, but it would have to do. I might be back home in half an hour, licking my wounds! The timing also had to be right. It would take some time to drive to her home on the farm close to the American border and then travel to Pilot Mound in time for the show, but not too early. Boy, this was complicated! Thankfully, she was at home (not on another date), and after a moment's delay, accepted my invitation! Years later, she would tell me that her hair had been up in curlers in preparation for church the next morning, but she improvised by removing the curlers and fashioning a ponytail. She wasn't going to pass up this date, she also confided much later. If she had realized the meticulous planning I'd undertaken, she might have accepted the date just to humour me! Apparently, she had always had a certain feeling for me since our earlier "fling" at age six or seven. She had often sent me Valentine cards when I was twelve to fifteen years of age. At that age, I was never impressed. But now, we had had our date. There would be many more. For now, a movie and a ride home, as no coffee shops were open. Judy carried the conversation. No shyness on her part, for which I was thankful.

The next year, 1962, would be a very difficult year for our family. My sister Linda passed away in June. She'd had two bouts with cancer, the first one at nine years of age, and now, the second at fifteen. Our whole family spent a Monday afternoon with her in the Winnipeg hospital to say our final goodbyes. Mom and Dad stayed with her, and the next day she died. Those of us at home were waiting for a phone call. We hadn't finished seeding, and I spent the day—my first time seeding—on a fifty-acre field on Beth's quarter, which was the farthest from our yard. Dad had given me some instructions as to how to set the drill for flax. My thoughts were on my work, but mostly on what was happening in that hospital room. In the late afternoon, a car approached me as I reached the end of the field. It was our neighbour, Peter Thiessen. He told me Linda had passed away. We were quiet for some time, and then he offered to take me home. I declined his offer. I needed an hour or so to finish the field, and I didn't know what I would do at home. Our family life had changed. We would miss our dear sister and daughter. None in our family had experienced a death so close to us. Mom and Dad were late coming home, so I didn't see them till the next morning. I remember Mom saying that she wished she had never had children. She was heartbroken, yet funeral planning needed to happen. A little more than a day after Linda's death, Raymond John was born! Elfrieda and Jake were parents, my folks were grandparents, and David and I had become uncles. These two events were too close together. How can a family mourn and celebrate at the same time?

The second difficulty that summer were the two hailstorms within a week of each other that totally destroyed our crop. Dad didn't carry hail insurance those years, so a lot of financial adjustments needed to be made. The rented land was rented on shares, so the landowners also suffered a loss. To make up for the loss, Dad did a lot of custom swathing and combining that fall. The farmers who hadn't suffered the storm had a bumper crop and readily hired the additional harvest help. Several were generous in their payments to Dad, recognizing the loss we had suffered.

That fall, the road past our farm was being prepared to be paved with asphalt. A large crew had set up a camp just across the creek from our yard. The work entailed the hauling of gravel onto the new highway, spreading it out, and then endless packing. I easily got a job driving a John Deere tractor pulling three packers. I was the middle of the three units doing this job. I knew how to drive a tractor, but this was different from field work. First of all, we travelled at a very slow speed. Secondly, one had to be very gentle in engaging the clutch. The rear tractor wheels shouldn't spin and create a little gouge on the road. It needed to be a smooth surface. Thirdly, we'd pack maybe a quarter mile at a time, travelling back and forth until the foreman was satisfied. One didn't readily see the progress we were making, and it was very boring. When doing field work on the farm, one would easily see the progress: five to six acres of discing done every hour. But the pay was good. I was making $1.30 an hour and working twelve to fourteen hours a day, five-and-a-half days a week. After two weeks on the job, I bought my first car. A trucker working on the project offered me his 1950 Ford, which was in pretty good shape for $160.00. Now I had my own car for dating and a paycheque to fund the dates!

The next two years produced good crops with favourable weather. Dad and his brother, my Uncle John, rented 960 acres of cropland on the American border and formed a partnership arrangement to farm this together. With that came a further upgrade in equipment: an eighty horsepower John Deere "4020," along with a "96" John Deere pull-type combine. These would prove to be Dad's last purchases and would serve him well until his retirement. I was somewhat dismayed by his decisions. "Why don't you let me rent some of this land? I need a start in farming." But to no avail. I contributed all my labour and received a bit of a wage at the end of the season. It was by no means an hourly wage like I'd received on the highway crew!

I did some odd jobs in the winters. A few farmers in the Clearwater area needed chore relief for a few days in the winter, and Dad volunteered my services. I'd milk some cows and harness up teams I wasn't familiar with. Every farm was different in procedure yet somewhat the same. I never heard any complaints. During the winter of 1964–65, I had a more regular job on the farm of Warren Fallis, who had several hundred head of cattle. The pay was $6.00 a day if I boarded with them and slightly more if I went home at night. I guess Dad must have fed my sheep when I didn't come home during the coldest days of the winter.

Another job I undertook was the assembling of equipment. Farmers could purchase equipment fully assembled or save money by assembling it themselves. It became my job to assemble a number of discers, a mower, as well as a rake, during the years of helping Dad. Dad saved the money, and I did the work! We were in an informal partnership arrangement, and I was okay with it. I would follow the step-by-step assembly instructions that were provided. I learned not to ignore the steps. If one did, one would later have to do some disassembling! I learned that if one could read and follow instructions, one could do many jobs that one would otherwise have to hire others to do. This served me well throughout life.

Meanwhile, Judy and I were able to spend more time together. She was teaching in local country schools after obtaining her teaching certificate in 1962–63 at the Teachers' College in Winnipeg. We both attended youth events in our church as well as sang in the church choir, with regular Friday evening practices. These were all a kind of date. I would often pick her up, since I now had my own "wheels!" We did have some special dates, like a Sunday at the Peace Gardens and some events in Winnipeg. The Brandon Fair was also a popular annual summer event. Judy treated me to a "Sadie Hawkins" date one year. She bought tickets for a Blue Bombers game in which the Bombers won over Calgary. I mention the win to confirm that I was paying attention to the game! By the summer of 1964, we both knew we were moving toward marriage, though we may not have verbalized this to each other.

If that were the case, we would need a home and a farm. Lorne Stewart wanted to sell the farm Dad had been renting, but he was asking a high price. When we indicated to him that his price was too high, he searched out other potential buyers and did secure one who had some interest, but I couldn't let this option go. We knew the farm. It was right next door, so Dad and I could farm together. It had a large, well kept home. Dad and I went over one evening to seriously make an offer. We agreed on the price of $42,000.00. Dad still thought it was too high, and he managed to talk Lorne into some concessions. There was a large harvest coming, and there was a shortage of granary space, so he convinced Lorne to buy some new bins. (He had never added any buildings to the farm since taking over from his father!) We shook hands and agreed to contact the lawyer, C. D. Treble, to draw up the sale. I was relieved.

The next morning, we got a call from the Stewarts that the deal was off. Mrs. Stewart, who had been present the evening before and never offered a comment, had voiced frustration concerning the concessions her husband had agreed to. I was devastated! What to do now? We had been so close. By evening, I informed Dad that I would go back to the Stewarts and offer their price with no concessions. Dad didn't think I'd succeed. I went, however, and made my offer, explaining that I wanted to get married and farm their land. After some thought, Florence turned to her husband and asked, "Should we sell our farm to Ernie?" He nodded his head yes. We agreed to go to the lawyer in a month's time, as he was presently on holidays. I went home and informed my parents of our agreement. Dad didn't think it would last. I said I was confident that it would. A month later, the meeting with the lawyer took place. Dad made a down payment of $10,000.00, and the Stewarts held the mortgage on the balance. I would make annual payments with interest set at 5 per cent on the mortgage. I'd pay Dad annual interest but wouldn't need to make principal payments.

With this purchase completed, the future looked more certain. Before Christmas, 1964, I proposed marriage to Judy on the staircase of the house that would become our home. We later set the date for the wedding as July 31. This would be after haying season and before the harvest of our first crop! Seeding that first crop was a special feeling. I believe that Dad must have paid for my share of the crop inputs, since I had little cash reserves. I would later reimburse him when I had some income.

Wedding plans filled the summer. The week before the wedding, Mom informed me that my grandmother was determined to boycott the wedding. She would not attend! Her son was to be our officiating minister, and we had asked him to conduct the wedding ceremony in English. That was the issue for my grandmother. She happened to be picking raspberries in our garden one morning, and I told Mom I'd go and talk to her. Mom didn't think it would help. She thought she knew her mother! I approached my grandmother in the raspberry patch, and in German asked her to come to our wedding. She told me she didn't understand English, and I explained that my German was very poor, since I hardly ever used that language. She looked me in the eye and said she would come! I went in and told Mom of her mother's change of mind. Mom was very surprised! I kind of got the sense that I had some strength in negotiations. First, I had persuaded the Stewarts to sell me their farm, and now I had persuaded my grandmother, in German, to attend our wedding!

The next challenge was to persuade the local banker to lend me some cash on a short term to finance our honeymoon trip. I had no cash left. I told my mom I had to go to town for this reason, and she informed me that I would receive some cash from Dad as a wedding gift, so there was no need to consult the banker. Sure enough, on the day of the wedding, she handed me an envelope. On it she had written, "No need to count. The are twenty twenties." Four hundred dollars! That was enough for our trip to the Black Hills in South Dakota as well as several months of living expenses upon our return. By then, some crop would have been sold and lambs sent to market. We were on our way!

Farming and married life were exciting! On the farm, I set about implementing some of the dreams I had since completing the diploma course. We needed to design a new farmstead. The existing barnyard and grain storage were down the slope from the house, closer to the creek. The plan was to move the barnyard south of the house onto an area level with the rest of the yard. I plowed up strips of ground to prepare for the planting of a shelterbelt the following year. I planned for a location for a granary and also a site for a future barn with the associated corrals. There would be good drainage on this site. The plans were for a flock of sheep, over two hundred in number. This required alfalfa to be planted, which would be the winter feed for the sheep. The alfalfa would be good for the land and, over the years, would be rotated to additional fields. We were pretty ambitious. We were in our first stage of life that Richard Rohr, the mystic, calls the establishment of the ego!

As our farm plans progressed, so did our family. Judy and I had discussed family size during courtship and had concluded, I think, that four was a nice size. Rhonda was born on June 12, 1966, on a beautiful Sunday morning. Fathers were just starting to be allowed to be present at the births, and the plan was that I would be there. However, without much explanation, I was excluded in the last hours. Dr. Irving later said that the first birth could be unpredictable, so he thought it wise the father not be present, even though I had attended the required sessions to prepare for this event. Rhonda was a delightful child with all kinds of creative play, some of which she learned from watching *Mr. Dressup* on TV. She loved the lambs in the barn, but one day she was butted by the ram! She was very upset! This didn't stop her, however, from coming out to the barn regularly.

Rhonda, Michelle, and Duane 1971

Michelle was born on January 3, 1968. It was one of the coldest periods of the winter, and I believe that week still features some record all time lows! She was a New Year's baby in the local hospital and was born as Canada started her second century! She came in second when she was entered in a baby contest at the fair that summer. There were a pile of babies entered! I also missed her birth. Our doctor was in the hospital as a patient himself recovering from a heart attack. He was prepared to assist with the birth and was to be called a few moments before the birth, but under the circumstances, he had no patience with having a father in the room.

Michelle joined her older sister and enjoyed riding the tricycle in circles through the downstairs rooms of our farmhouse. She became a great companion to her older sister and had a wonderful imagination. She learned to ride a bike when she was quite young. Rhonda had received two bikes for her sixth birthday, so Michelle "inherited" one. I recall assisting her first ride by holding the back of the bike as she pedalled down our lane. On the way back, I let go, and she was on her own. When she noticed this, she started to scream! I wonder if our Tiessen neighbours heard her! She could pedal but didn't know how to stop! Somehow, she managed.

Duane was born on October 17, 1969. I took Judy to be admitted to the hospital during the afternoon and was told it would be a while before the birth would happen. I wouldn't be attending this birth either. Dr. Irving had passed away and the new Spanish doctor had no sympathy for the trend of fathers being present at births. Since I was of no use at the hospital, I went to the bank to do some business. The manager noticed me and called me into his office, telling me he needed an updated status of our financial situation. He started by inquiring as to the size of our family. How many children? I was stumped. I said that when I entered the bank we had two, but by now, it could be three! He chuckled and said he'd mark down three!

We now had two girls and a boy. Toy tractors and trucks became favourite toys. During the spring when he was two-and-a-half years old, he'd meet me when I'd come to the yard with the tractor for lunch. I'd head for the house to eat, and he'd climb up on the tractor seat and sit there until I was finished lunch. This became a regular pattern. One day I came back to the tractor and Duane had greased it! The grease gun had been on the tractor, and he found out that he could squeeze the trigger and spread grease all over the dash and the gauges, as well as a film of grease on every lever he could find. The steering wheel too! His face and clothes hadn't escaped the grease job. I called Judy to come and get him. She'd have a job cleaning him up, as I'd have a job with the tractor. I was upset and reprimanded him sharply. I can still see the confused and pained expression on his face, in spite of the grease. In his mind, he had been helping me. I'd like to think that if it had happened when I was older, I'd have laughed and maybe even asked Judy to bring the camera! After wiping off all of his handiwork, I was back to the field. Later that afternoon, I needed to operate another lever I hadn't used till then, and my hand became covered with grease. I had missed cleaning a spot that he had discovered! Well, he had created a memory!

Life was busy on the farm. We were growing crops, raising lambs, gardening, erecting new buildings, as well as raising a family. A lot of it was hard labour. The thousands of square bales required by the sheep for winter feed were all handled by hand. First, they were stooked in piles of ten behind the baler. Then when the baling was completed, they were loaded onto racks with the front-end loader and hauled to the yard. Then they were placed on the bale elevator and arranged by hand to fashion a stack. In the winter, these bales would be moved by hand again and placed in feeders for the sheep. I was in good physical shape!

Another component to our life was the financial aspect. We had long-term loans that needed to be managed. Funds required for operating the farm as well as living expenses. Income wasn't regular, so we had to manage the bank accounts to get through the times between sales. One winter there was a gap in sales, and our bank account dwindled to zero. We had grain to sell, but there were no quotas calling for grain to be delivered, and the local elevators were all full as well. Flax was a cash crop but had all been sold. I didn't consider selling some of the sheep as breeding stock, since these sheep were producers for the next year's income. We needed groceries. I didn't consider asking Dad for a loan, as I suspected he would have told me I should be milking cows for a regular weekly cream cheque.

My only option was to ask the banker for a short-term loan. Before going to the bank, I stopped at the post office to get the mail. Imagine my surprise when I saw the cheque for the final payment for wool I had sold the previous summer! I had forgotten about this money I had coming, but one never knew when it would arrive. I checked some of my old account books and determined that the cheque would have been around $50.00. This proved to be enough for us to get through the next while until some grain could be sold.

Farming, Married with Children

A few years ago, over a family meal where all of our family was gathered, I asked our kids if they had ever experienced poverty. They were young adults, some with spouses and kids of their own. Some had been university students for several years, but none claimed a time when they were really poor. I told them my story. Some time later, I was curling in a bonspiel in Clearwater and was having lunch with a senior curler and farmer from north of Mather. There were just the two of us at the table, and I asked him about experiencing poverty. I told him my story and the discussion with my children. He chuckled and told me his own story. He and his wife, way back in time, had loaded up their family and set out to visit extended family about one hundred miles away. He had checked his wallet and had less than $4.00, so he stopped at the bank in Crystal City to withdraw a few more dollars. The teller informed him that his account was overdrawn and proceeded to take half of the money the farmer had in his wallet! They still went on their journey and only experienced one flat tire! They patched the tube themselves, so there was no expense. Quite a story. More dramatic than my own!

Our life was about to change … a change that we would not have anticipated when we were first married. A major decision was pending.

(I wonder if I've been too unfair to my dad, as he's not here to defend himself. In many ways, I experienced him as not being supportive enough in assisting me to get established in farming. I had always anticipated that my ten plus years of supplying him with farm labour would result in more support later on. But we never discussed these aspects and expectations. He had started his own farming with little support, so I suppose he thought I could as well. Over the years, he did lend us sizable loans with interest. He provided the down payment on the farm, on which I paid only annual interest. When I informed him fifteen years later that I would start paying back the principal, he informed me that he would cancel the loan. This was a gift. On two occasions, he lent us short-term loans when we were making property purchases and needed bridge funding. He and Mom also left their family a generous inheritance.)

Major Decision Time

One day last summer I said to Judy, "The two best decisions we made were to leave the farm and to come back to the farm!" If I had told her the two best decisions that *I* had made, I would have said they were marrying her and having a family! (To have a family, however, had also been a joint decision.)

The decision to leave the farm was not made easily or quickly. I truly liked farming and country life and always thought it would be my lifelong vocation. The first seven years on our own farm were not without challenges. The farm economy took a downturn, and crop yields weren't great. Prices for wheat, barley, and flax tanked in 1968 and remained there. It was taking some time to establish a productive flock. Lamb and wool prices, while stable, were not rewarding. There entered some disillusionment on my part. I couldn't see an option to expand our land base, and I didn't have my own machinery other than the haying equipment. I found myself checking out off-farm employment to supplement the farm income. I did have my Diploma in Agriculture, so I'd be employable in agri-business. It was difficult to envision how I could manage two jobs. The one was keeping me busy.

At the same time, I was getting more involved in our church. I'd been teaching Sunday school to a large group of high school fellows, and I guess I was exhibiting some gifts that led me to be selected as one in a group of three to preach an occasional sermon. This would supplement the work of the two lay ministers who served our congregation. Due to this involvement and experience, I began to wonder if pastoral ministry might be an option for me. But immediately I faced a barrier: it would require theological training. I would not pursue this path without study, as I knew so little. Up to this point, our church had elected local members to the pulpit, and theological training wasn't a prerequisite. But things were changing. Some congregations in the province were moving to salaried positions and required college, and in some cases, seminary training. I hadn't even completed high school, and I couldn't envision myself back there for a year.

Later, I was informed that I could enroll in college as a mature student. The first year was a trial, and if a certain grade level was achieved, the mature status would be removed and I could continue as a regular student. I thought about this a lot as I contemplated our future. I needed to share this idea to Judy, which I did at some point. Could we leave the farm, study for three years, and seek a salaried position in a Mennonite church somewhere in our national conference of churches? I don't recall her exact reaction, even though she'd had no idea of the thinking I'd been doing. Her reaction wasn't negative, and she wasn't reluctant to test out the possibilities. We would pursue this option together and see where it would take us. Later, she would say that while she hadn't seen it coming, it seemed almost a natural projection.

At the time, I thought of our possible venture as a "call." That was church language. We were taught in church to be open to being "called by God." It was reassuring in many ways. I never heard any voice from above, but I had received several messages from friends and neighbours. They had detected some gifts and affirmed them. It was interesting that these also came from outside our (still largely closed) Mennonite community. On one occasion I had spoken in the local United Church during their Sunday service, promoting an upcoming inter-denominational event. I was greeted by people after the service, and Doug Campbell, a local bachelor farmer, shook my hand and said, "You've missed your calling." In my mind, he was an unlikely person to pronounce an affirmation like that. The editor of the local paper had also been at the service. While I was in his office some time later, he told me he had the gift of using words in his paper but couldn't speak in public. He told me that I had that gift. These words, unexpected affirmation, along

Major Decision Time

with our own struggle for direction, urged us along in our decision making. Had farming run its course? Was some form of ministry our future? A call?

I didn't play up the notion that I was a great guy because God was calling me out of the sheep fold, like King David of old, into his service! I rather saw the human dimension. We have choices in life and a variety of gifts, abilities, and interests. We can do different things as we live our lives, and change can be good. Later I saw the process of being called by the three churches I served in a similar way. I didn't spend hours on my knees, seeking the perfect match. Rather, I trusted the system. Some congregations were seeking leadership. Some people had training that might meet the needs of that group. Let's get together to see if there might be a potential match that could lead us to proceed. Check with trusted advisers for their view on the match. Pray. Eventually, the congregation issues an invitation, and the person is free to respond. It seems to have worked in our experience. I believe that all three congregations were good matches. I recall an acquaintance of mine sharing his experience of determining whether a potential move to Swift Current might be God's call for him. As he finished praying, he glanced out the window and a large transport truck passed by on the street. Painted on the side was "Swift Current Transport." That, for him, was his sign. To each his own, I suppose. Sad to say, the move didn't end up being that positive. He moved again.

Since retirement, I see another side of our decision. We may simply have been early victims of a poor farm economy. Farming long term seemed unattainable. We needed an option, and pastoral ministry was a viable option. Since that time (early 1970s), the farming landscape has been altered considerably. (Almost all small farms with three hundred to six hundred acres have disappeared. They were just too economically fragile.) Today, one thousand acres is considered to be a small farm. This size of farm would require a working spouse to make a viable living. This causes me to reconsider. Judy was a trained teacher. She was offered and accepted a term position in the local school the first fall of our marriage, as the regular teacher was on a medical leave for a few months. When that leave was extended for the year, Judy was offered the contract for the whole year. We declined that option, as we couldn't envision getting our car started every morning through a cold winter and making sure the road to the highway was clear of snow. Roads could be blocked for a week after a storm. Off-the-farm working spouses were not the norm. Currently, with good cars, well-plowed roads, and daycare options, no one would turn down such an opportunity. This might have allowed us to remain on the farm. A few weeks later, we discovered we were expecting our first child! Pregnant!

Back to the story. Judy and I agreed to consider the change of vocation … it would have been the early months of 1971. We decided to take a course on the biblical book of Acts that was being offered in our church by a faculty member of Elim Bible School. It wasn't quite college level, but it would serve as a test of my studying ability. Judy got high marks, but mine weren't as high but quite acceptable. Next was the choice of a college. I was inclined to test out Winnipeg Bible College, situated southeast of Winnipeg. I understood this school to be inter-denominational, which I thought meant it would encompass Mennonite, Catholic, and Protestant faith perspectives. I discovered it was rather non-denominational, or a denomination of its own. We visited the campus and met with the president—a youthful, energetic man who was very friendly and welcoming. What I recall most about our visit was that he carefully pointed out the difference between premillennialism and post millennialism, and which one his college favoured—or in fact, was the correct view in his mind! That didn't impress me, but I stored the information in my brain to re-visit later on.

Our next visit was to Canadian Mennonite Bible College in Winnipeg, which was our church college. I was familiar with this school but also aware of some people back home who declared its teaching to be flawed. Here I also met with the president, an older gentleman with a kindly spirit, Dr. Poettker. After considering the purpose of our visit and our vision of preparing for future work in ministry, he asked me if we owned a farm. When I replied in the affirmative, he advised me, "Don't sell it!" He must have encountered other young farmers like me looking for change, and when studies didn't work out, they had no option but to go back to the farm. My thought, however, was that he didn't know me and how confident I was of our plans. What Dr. Poettker didn't realize at the time was that he was giving us financial advice. Little did anyone know that the under $100.00 per acre I had paid in 1964 would be worth $3,000.00 per acre in 2015. This would be our retirement fund!

Major Decision Time

Back to our college choice. CMBC had housing for married students on campus. This was definitely a plus for us. We viewed the two-bedroom units and had a brief visit with Ron and Connie Loeppky, whom we would encounter later on our journey. This place became our choice. I had asked Victor Sawatsky, the Elim instructor, about our college options, and he'd advised me to first attend CMBC. If I didn't like it, it would be easier to transfer credits to WBC than the other way around. I realized later his advice was sneaky. He had gotten to know us and knew that if we started at CMBC, we wouldn't transfer after a year. We applied and I was accepted as a mature student. The college had an agreement with the University of Manitoba to cross register certain courses that would apply toward a BA. This was also where the mature status applied. A major decision finalized! It's really rather comical to me. I was a mature student due to my age (twenty-eight), but I sure wasn't mature in my faith development. Rather very naive. But then, one is naive most of one's life if one is committed to lifelong learning!

There was still the farming to wrap up, but it was time to tell our parents of our plans. Up until this point, we hadn't told anyone. We were charting our own way. Both sets of parents lived in the community, and our three children were their grandchildren. Judy's parents were supportive. Her dad offered some words of encouragement. He valued pastoral work. The several personal words he spoke to me were more than he was usually capable of expressing. He was much more at home helping with a difficult lamb delivery, or butchering for us, or any other physical labour. I appreciated his few words. Mom was quiet, possibly pondering her only grandchildren moving far away. Extended family life was strong. My dad's immediate response was that he couldn't see how we could swing it financially: "You won't make it," he claimed. I told him I could see myself through the next years. When in the process of farming year after year, one keeps putting revenue from one crop just harvested into the next crop. When you cease farming, this isn't the case. We had accumulated some net worth. Instead of baling hay for the next winter, I sold the alfalfa as a standing crop to the Hudsons. We would dispose of our sheep flock, and we had our haying equipment and a tractor to sell. There were bank loans to repay, but this could be done while still leaving enough to see us at least part way through three years of study. It was also our intention to come back after our first winter to seed one more crop and gather the harvest. I'm not sure if he was convinced, but he didn't try to discourage us further. Later, he confessed that he had seen our move coming, so it wasn't a complete surprise. He had noted my interest and my abilities expressed in our church.

At this point of history in Mennonite farming circles, there were two acceptable occupations for men: farming and ministry. For women, it was teaching or nursing up until marriage. Then mothering and homemaking. I don't recall if Mom said anything. In Dad's company, she wouldn't offer strong opinions too readily. She had years earlier encouraged me not to farm. After my accident, my right eye would constantly tear due to the surgery, so after a day's tillage work in the fields, my face would be a mess, with dirt crusted around my eye and most of my face. Mom would say, "Ernie, get off the farm and get a job in the city." Of course, I wouldn't hear of it at the time. So maybe she was okay with our plan. She also had three of Elfrieda and Jakie's children as her grandchildren, and they appeared well rooted in the community!

I'd had an offer since the spring to buy the whole flock of sheep. It seemed like a sincere offer, and no deposit was requested or offered to secure the deal. When I phoned him in July to make arrangements, he informed me that he had changed his mind. I was stuck with 250 sheep, no winter feed, no buyer, and six weeks until our departure. If all else failed, I'd have to sell them through the Winnipeg auction at well below the price for a breeding flock. I placed an ad in the *Manitoba Co-operator,* and lo and behold, a call came from Paris, Ontario. I hadn't expected the ad to reach outside Manitoba. George German asked about the flock and, when satisfied, made arrangements to come out by bus the following week. We picked him up in town, and within a few hours the deal was finalized. He made arrangements for trucking the sheep to Austin, Manitoba, and from there they would be loaded on a CPR livestock car. While waiting for these plans to materialize, he travelled further west for a few days into Saskatchewan. On the long weekend of August 1971, the sheep were loaded, and our yard seemed empty. No sounds of sheep after six years. Sadness was experienced, as well as relief that this change of buyer had happened in such a short time frame. Harvest was yet to come, and then we would be on our way.

Major Decision Time

There was some rain the weekend before we had planned to move, so we decided to move a truckload of furniture to our apartment at CMBC and spend a few days in the space we would inhabit for the next few years. With the truck loaded and the family waiting in the car, I sat down on the concrete steps at our east entrance and pondered: *What have we planned? What steps have we put in motion?* A moment of doubt. It seemed so permanent. No turning back. I consider the concrete steps to symbolize permanence. They had been there since 1905 and would be there till 1994. I was moving off these steps, and I had no one to blame but myself. I had intended to farm at this place all my life. Judy came back from the car. The kids were restless. She asked what was keeping me. I wiped a tear and said, "Coming." I wouldn't have suggested at that point that this move would later be viewed as our first best decision.

As a consequence of this decision, we spent the next three winters in Winnipeg on the campus of CMBC at the edge of the Charleswood Forest. This wasn't a bad place to be for a farm family. We were about as close to the country as one could be in this city. Our apartment was a two-bedroom suite on the basement level of the residence. A number of married couples, some with children, also lived there. We readily made friends and enjoyed a social life, creating lifelong friendships in some cases. The two girls needed to share a bedroom, which was a change for them. They'd had separate rooms in the large, old home we had left. In some ways, life was like camping! It was such a change and a bit of a relief for me not to be responsible for running a whole farming operation.

The first fall was very busy. We went back to the farm every weekend until the end of October to complete the harvest, do the fall tillage, clean up the garden, and prepare the house to be unoccupied for the winter. Rhonda started kindergarten in Winnipeg at a school within walking distance. A number of older students also attended who could walk with her. I was being oriented to classes, reading, and working at class assignments. I hadn't written essays in high school.

It was a relief when the trips back to the farm ceased and we could relax on the weekends in Winnipeg. We decided to attend Fort Garry Mennonite Fellowship as our church. We knew a few people who belonged to this congregation, and we found a warm welcome. This would be our church home for the next three years. A pattern developed during that time. One Sunday on our way back to our apartment from church, we stopped at Kentucky Fried Chicken and ordered a bucket of chicken and fries as take-out. What a treat! After that, it was difficult to drive past that place without stopping! We didn't do it weekly, but over the years the meals must have added up.

The first year went by quickly, and in spring we were back on the farm for one final crop. That season while on the tractor for the many hours, I realized for the first time how lonely farming was. I had spent eight months in an intense setting surrounded by people, and now I was spending twelve hours a day on the tractor. It did give me time to process the information that had been pumped into my brain over the past winter. I also read a book, *Call to Faithfulness*, which contained a series of articles written by the CMBC faculty. Some of the writers had been my profs. This reading and processing began to come together to prepare for me for the next year. I'd had some doubt as to whether I was "catching on" to theological thinking.

The summer was spent on the farm (without the sheep), and it was soon time for the harvest. The procedure was much like the year before, with several trips back to the farm after the college and school year had started. Finally, the fall work was completed, and we turned the cropland over to Judy's brother, Harvey, who would rent our farm starting the next year. He would work this land for the next forty years!

Two more years at CMBC followed. Judy was able to take some courses there, as well as edit and type all of my course essays. Michelle entered kindergarten. She was ready for it, as she was a January baby and had to wait for an extra year. Duane had his friends and enjoyed riding his trike down the long hall in the winters. In the spring and fall, we would ride our bikes to the Assiniboine Park for an outing. The girls had their bikes, and Duane rode in the seat for kids mounted on the back of my bike.

I had been asked to preach in the Carman Mennonite Church once a month during my second year. They were without a pastor, so they made this arrangement with two of us from CMBC. That spring, we moved to Carman, as they had asked me to come on full time for the four summer months. We moved into a tiny house provided by the congregation. This meant that Rhonda had to switch schools in grade one. She rode her bike all the way across town by herself after I had accompanied her on the first few days.

This was my first venture in being a pastor. I met some of the other clergy in town at a ministerial meeting, and I recall the Anglican priest telling me that the basic requirement for clergy in his denomination was to be able to read English! My Mennonites required considerably more! He also said that if his congregation got a little too uptight about something, he would organize a wine and cheese evening, and all would settle down! I was learning things I hadn't been taught at college! Over the years to come, I appreciated the clergy I met from different traditions, sharing perspectives we differed on and others we held in common. And a lot of clergy humour!

I wasn't totally comfortable with the "pastor" label. One morning I was having coffee with a parishioner at the co-op and was introduced to someone who'd stopped by to chat at our table. He asked what I was doing in town, and I told him I worked at the church just down the street.

"What kind of work?" he asked. "Painting?"

I guess I didn't dress like a pastor and wasn't yet comfortable introducing myself as one.

The third year culminated in my graduation at the end of April. We had a big celebration with our families, and I felt good about my accomplishments. I had completed all the course requirements and had finished the three years of study without any debt! In fact, we bought a new car that spring with cash. Some of the 1972 crop was still available to sell in January of 1974. We also received final payments from the Canadian Wheat Board for the 1972 wheat and barley sales. Grain prices had improved remarkably, and we benefited from this increase. The car served us well for the next ten years—no repair bills! We were ready to move on yet regretted leaving the place where we had experienced such good relationships.

We would be moving to Osler, Saskatchewan, in August to serve as pastor of the Mennonite church in that community. Two couples from there had come to my grad to support us, and they served as a bridge for me from being a student to becoming a pastor. We decided to stay in Winnipeg for the next few months so as not to disrupt school for Rhonda and Michelle. I found work in a factory in north Winnipeg but changed jobs after a few weeks when I was asked to serve as Mennonite chaplain in the Winnipeg hospitals, as the regular chaplain had requested a break. This ended up being good training for me. It was an eye-opener to visit two men who had spent almost twenty years in their "iron lungs." They were polio victims from the Morden area. They had more to tell me than what I could offer them.

July was spent holidaying at Crystal City with parents, as well as camping with friends at local resorts. We were saying goodbye and would be leaving the province. We packed up our household goods on two trucks. Mom and Dad drove our loaded one-ton truck, and Judy's brothers drove their three-ton truck loaded to the top. (We had our three kids packed in our car, with the trunk packed as well.) By late afternoon, we all arrived in Osler!

West to Osler, Saskatchewan

We arrived in Osler in early August 1974. It was three months since CMBC graduation and six months since the decision had been made to come here as a pastor family.

How come Osler? It started at the Canadian Conference annual meeting in July 1973 in Edmonton, Alberta. We had one more year of college remaining. On the last morning of the conference, I was asked to speak a few words regarding my experience at CMBC during the college reporting period. There were likely seven hundred plus people in attendance. I had never spoken to a crowd that size before, but I managed to speak with just a few scribbled notes. I don't recall being nervous. Later that day, as the conference was drawing to a close, Rev. Henry Gerbrandt, Executive Secretary of the Conference, approached me and said a delegation from the Osler Mennonite Church had asked to meet me. We arranged a table and had a brief meeting.

They came right to the point and said they were in pastoral search for their congregation. They had heard me speak and felt I might be a fit for them. I told them we still had one year of study remaining, but they were okay with that. We were encouraged to stop by at Osler on our way home to Manitoba the next day. We did that and had a brief visit at the church and then lunch with Leonard and Marge at their farm home. Leonard was very organized and suggested a framework as to how we could proceed. I believe that within a month we gave our assent to proceed with exploring this opportunity with Osler. Information started flowing by mail, and then arrangements were made to have us as a family visit the congregation for a weekend of exploration. I would be the guest speaker for the Sunday worship service. This could make or break our future! No, this service was downplayed in significance. I was assured by the leadership that the sermon I would preach would not be the only consideration to being "called". So, just relax, and enjoy the moment!

We met with seniors and youth groups and toured the surrounding area. Mrs. Dyck, one of the senior widows, asked me if I could preach in German. When I told her I couldn't, she said that was okay. It was the younger people who were important and needed to hear the gospel! I hadn't expected that kind of a reply. My grandmother in Manitoba wouldn't have agreed. We were well hosted! We had meals with several families in some pretty fancy homes. We wondered if we would fit in, as our economic standing was much lower, especially after three years of study. We were invited to have breakfast the morning of our departure with Art and Edna. They lived in a small house some distance from the village. It was out of our way, but we agreed to come. And we were glad we did. The kitchen was small, so the table was pulled out from the wall. Our three children sat on a bench and enjoyed a great meal. We realized that not all members of the church lived on the same scale. We believe this visit clinched it for us. If the congregation would vote in January to confirm a call, we would agree to come!

Now we were here. We had toured the three-bedroom parsonage on our previous visit and had been told that some work would be done on it before fall. A new garage with cement carport and sidewalks greeted us upon arrival. The interior of the house had been freshly painted and new carpeting installed ! What luxury! We started unloading our furniture. It looked shabby coming off the truck, so I said to take it to the basement. I suddenly realized that everything might end up in the basement. So we moved our stuff in. This was who we were.

We had two weeks to settle in before I'd officially start work. Our kids explored the neighbourhood and soon found friends. School wouldn't start for a month, so they could establish friendships before that. Rhonda and Michelle would walk to the elementary school, and Duane would be starting kindergarten. Several of the teachers in the school were members of our congregation, so our kids would be well looked after. Osler was a small, intimate Mennonite village. It was very different from Crystal City, where Mennonite families were a small minority when I started school. It was a safe place in many ways. The majority of our congregation were dairy farmers shipping bulk milk. Dairy had not been my favourite farm enterprise, but these people were experts in this business. Several dairy farmers would nod off during morning worship services, as they had been up since 5:00 a.m.

I had some difficulty adapting to the work of a pastor. In my first weeks in the church office, I would note the grain trucks coming into town to the elevator. Harvest was in full swing, and I was missing it. I had participated in twenty harvests, from ten years of age till thirty. Pastoral work didn't seem to be real work, so it took some time to adjust. I shared this thought with Mr. Neudorf, a retired farmer and local historian. He was surprised by my comment and assured me that ministerial work was of utmost importance. I'm not sure if I was convinced.

One of the largest dairy farms in the valley was the Martens' dairy. I stopped by during milking one day and got to meet the grandfather who had started this farm that was now operated by his two sons. One of the sons was a member of our congregation. His father adhered to a more conservative Mennonite church. He told me that day in the barn that farming was the most important occupation on God's earth, and he took great pride in the food he had produced in his lifetime. Then he reconsidered and looked at me, knowing that I was a minister, and said, "Agriculture is very important, right next to the Bible!" What a character! He spoke this in Low German, and I understood enough of the language to get every word. A few years later, the Martens family hosted a large gathering meant to showcase their cattle and barns. They sold a lot of breeding stock, so this gathering included people from all over the province. Harry had asked me if I would help them that day, without specifying what my job would be. When I came, he gave me a shovel and asked me to patrol the length of the barn and scrape off any manure (shit) that had been expelled and not reached the gutter. The cows were all tied up in stanchions. Heaven forbid if a cow would lie down in her own mess and soil her carefully groomed white and black body! I did that all day. Likely the lowest person on the proverbial totem pole! I took some delight that the visitors didn't realize that I was a local minister, and I respected Harry for enlisting me for this task, not thinking that it might be beneath my dignity.

The second struggle I encountered the first year or two was the move from an academic setting to congregational life. I had learned so much at college and enjoyed vigorous academic debate. Bible, theology, and history were my specialties. But was this of interest to the farmers, mothers, labourers in this congregation? We were visiting with a farm (dairy) family one Sunday who had joined the congregation several years previous, coming from a more conservative setting. While touring the farmyard with the father, he told me how much he appreciated the national church paper, *The Canadian Mennonite*. (This paper changed titles several times. Might have been different at that time.) He stated that he found the articles very interesting and thought provoking. I was being enlightened! I had another similar experience with Joe, who was committed to his dairy. He hadn't missed a milking for many years. He was one who would nod off in church at times! Visiting the family, also on a Sunday afternoon, he said, "Ernie, there are three sermons over the past while that were especially meaningful to me." Then he listed the themes. I was blown away! People were listening. We were connecting. An experience like this can empower one for quite some time.

Life at Osler was busy. Judy was also adapting to being a pastor's wife. She occasionally has reminded me that she thought she had married a farmer! But she was a natural, meeting people easily and both of us became adept at quickly learning people's names and remembering them. Much hosting took place. Friends and relatives visited from Manitoba, usually on weekends. We added Jason to the family on May 13, 1975, much to the delight of the three older children as well as Mom and Dad! Good friends of ours from CMBC ended up in a church within a thirty-minute drive from Osler. They added a fourth child the same year. I joked that the Saskatchewan Government required "immigrants" entering the province to have an additional child within a year. This was a policy meant to reverse the population drain that was being experienced!

Judy had started labour early on a Sunday morning, so I took her to City Hospital in Saskatoon. But I needed to be back in church that morning. A child dedication service was scheduled for twelve infants/children. There was a backlog, since the congregation had been without a pastor for over two years. I performed this service with the thought that we could have a little one before I got back to the city! I'm not sure how I managed. The labour had stopped in the meanwhile, and Jason wasn't born till Tuesday! I had wanted to attend the birth, but the nurse who called me that morning said there was no rush, but it would happen sometime that morning. If Judy had been on the phone, she would have said to come right away! I arrived too late for the birth.

The dedication service was just one of several special services I had to learn to conduct. There were communion services, funerals, weddings, and baptisms. Each of these services was a new experience for me. The congregation must have realized that they were dealing with a rookie! Funerals were the most difficult. Conducting the service was one thing but learning how to provide pastoral care for the families was another. People were very understanding, for all were dealing with grief. There were difficult funerals. Accidental death. Death of an infant and a child.

Sermons were another matter. Term papers and essays were required at college, but sermons came due every seven days. And extensions were not granted! Very few resources were available. I needed to identify themes and scripture passages for each of the services, so I formed a way to outline options for the weeks ahead. When ideas formed, I would slot a brief outline of the idea and place it in my calendar. That way, I wasn't scrambling on a Friday to form a message for that Sunday. It worked for me. My preaching must have improved during our time at Osler, as a younger farmer commented on it. He was sincere. He meant to say that I had become a pretty good preacher, but I thought that when one starts at such a low point, it doesn't need to improve much to be better!

Pastoral life in this kind of a setting is intertwined with family life. We had an active household, and it was Judy who did 90 per cent of the parenting (my estimate). We did have family outings. We would go to the Bonanza restaurant in Saskatoon with friends from church many Sundays for the noon meal. The kids soon had their favourite meals. It was always a treat.

Several times over the years, we would meet our CMBC friends with their four children and book two rooms at the Sheraton Hotel in Saskatoon. The water slide and the kiddy pool created a fun weekend. We'd go with coolers full of food so we only needed to eat "out" once or twice over the two days we were there. We also purchased a used tent trailer that we could hardly afford. We used it for years. We towed it through the mountains to British Columbia on the way to attend the annual conference of our national church. In 1978, we towed it to Kansas, USA, for the Mennonite World Conference. We took our time travelling there and found excellent campsites. A routine developed as everyone pitched in to set up camp. Rhonda had a banana box full of books that she finished on that trip! Duane was ready to explore every place we stopped. Michelle entertained Jason along the way. While at the conference, Judy and Gayle kept us fed, making sandwiches for the next day every evening by the light of a lantern. I drove and plotted the route! Kansas was hot—110 degrees Fahrenheit the final day! Camping trips later within Saskatchewan and Manitoba might not have been as exciting but were always enjoyable family times. Breaks like that were needed by all of us.

Pastors live and work with people, and one needs to learn how to deal with conflict. A new Sunday school curriculum was being developed, and Judy was part of the team introducing this material to the congregations in the surrounding area. At Osler, it was shared during a Sunday worship service. The team was creative and acted out the story "The Giving Tree." It was well done, I thought, and demonstrated an approach to teaching children. The German Bible study group of seniors met the following week. I led this group in English. Scripture was read in German and discussion followed in three languages! But before the study could begin, Mr. Neudorf voiced a concern that had been discussed among all the seniors in the few days since the Sunday service. I was asked why I had allowed such a story to be told in church. "The Giving Tree" was not a biblical story, so was not suitable for children in church. And my wife was one of the persons acting it out! But that fact wasn't raised by the seniors.

I could have reacted in a very defensive way, but I didn't. The story was about a big tree that had provided all kinds of gifts to a young boy. A place to climb in the branches. Shade on a hot day. Fruit in season. When the boy became a man, he asked the tree for its trunk so that he could use the lumber to build a house. The tree consented and was left with just a stump. A very good story. I responded to the seniors' concern by reminding them that Jesus spoke in parables. He didn't tell Bible stories from the Old Testament. His stories were from nature so that people could understand. And Jesus welcomed children. The story was a parable. I was then asked what the story meant. I told them that the tree represented God. At the end, God gave his life! They now completely understood and could appreciate the story. However, this should have been explained at the service. Conflict settled!

Not all conflicts were successfully resolved. A group of four women confronted me one day as I was leaving the church. They had agreed to tell me that I shouldn't encourage women to express their gifts as much as I did. According to scripture, they told me, it was the men's role to teach and the women's role to listen. I responded by pointing out to them that they, as women, were telling me, a man and minister, how to interpret scripture. (They didn't catch the irony!) I then told them that were I to agree with them, I'd need to tell them that they were silly women and to go home and listen to their husbands! However, I reassured them that I didn't agree with their understanding. This was too complicated for them. This conflict was not well handled, and these families were not strong supporters. Years later, all these families had left the church for more "evangelical churches." Their issue wasn't just with me. I was long gone by then.

Churches lose members and also gain members. Over the decades, the percentage of people identifying with the church has declined significantly. In pioneering days, the percentage of people attending church could have been 90 per cent. In the twenty-first century, it's down to 20 per cent or lower. Osler Church had gained some of its members from the more conservative churches in the area. One family had decided to join years before we came, and the large family was very active and providing leadership. The father had chosen Osler Mennonite, I was told, because he wanted his children to experience a Sunday school. While I was pastor, some of this trend continued. Families would start attending and, sometime in the future, request to become formal members. I vividly remember one such occasion. I was visiting the family and inquired as to their reason for joining Osler Church. The response I got was not what I was expecting. The father said, "I like to curl, and my old church doesn't allow it!" Okay, I was back to reality! They were a solid family!

One summer we were away attending the Canadian Conference in British Columbia. When we got back, I was told that an Epp family had moved into the area and had attended the service at Osler that Sunday. I needed to pay them a pastoral visit and encourage them to choose Osler as their church. Edgar Epp had been recruited by MCC to take a position in the Saskatchewan office. Several Saskatoon churches were courting this family as well, so there was no time to waste. I reluctantly paid them a visit on their acreage the following week. Let them make up their own mind. How was I to formulate this invitation anyway? They were still in the process of moving in when I arrived, and Edgar had his head under the sink repairing a plumbing problem. I had introduced myself while he was working. When he finally surfaced, I made my pitch and excused myself, noting that they were busy getting settled in and it wasn't a good time for a visit. Anyway, they joined Osler and made a good contribution. At a congregational meeting when we were dealing with my resignation, Edgar spoke up to inform them of my unique style of recruiting new members. He told them that when he had finished with the sink and greeted me, I had pointed out the kitchen window and asked him if he knew who had lived across the highway on another acreage. He said it had been the Lobes. Then I had said, "Yes, the Vern Lobes. They had no trouble driving the six miles of gravel roads to attend Osler Mennonite, so it shouldn't be a deterrent to the Epps either." I had left it at that. Edgar stated that no other pastor had come close to my creative pitch! I would never have recalled this encounter if Edgar hadn't shared it.

One major community conflict would forever shape our Osler years. I will briefly mention it here but will attempt to deal with it more fully in another chapter. Land options were being secured for Eldorado Nuclear in the Warman area. The proposed refinery was creating a lot of uncertainty due to people not knowing what it was really about. This led to a community meeting in our church basement to address the issue. Little concrete information was available. At the end of the meeting, a number of people expressed interest in pursuing it further. This was the fall of 1976. In the next few months, the Warman & District Concerned Citizens Group was formed. I ended up becoming the chair of an executive committee made up of approximately a dozen people. Several were from our church, but it was in reality a community committee. Though I always felt supported by the church in my role, there were some that objected to their pastor being involved in what was deemed to be a political, not religious, activity. I often wondered why others involved from our congregation weren't being taken to task. The next years required a great deal of effort, which would culminate in three weeks of official hearings before a federal environmental panel. The larger community was overwhelmingly opposed to the refinery.

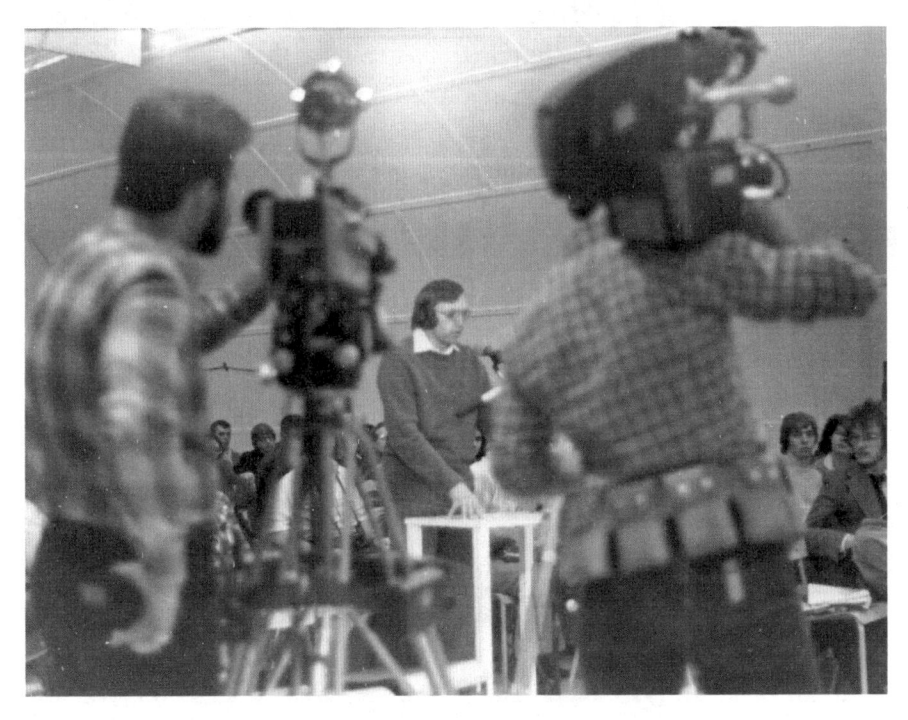

Uranium Refinery Hearings 1980

A unique aspect of this church was the number of young adults involved in it. Youth from the congregation had always been encouraged to attend the provincial Bible school situated in Swift Current after completing high school. The school at this time had an emphasis on stewardship and a simpler way of living. Young adults who had recently graduated, current students, and those planning on attending enjoyed getting together and discussing life's challenges. Since there was a core group at Osler, friends from further away often came to the Osler area on weekends to enjoy each other's company. This group often met at our home. Judy provided tasty snacks that were always appreciated and guaranteed return visits! (A few would stay till well after midnight on a Saturday. I would be leading worship the next morning short on sleep. Whatever!) Conversations produced fun and laughter and then the next moment utterly serious topics.

When the "Eldorado issue" became a factor in the community, this group took a lively interest. They were supportive of the efforts of the citizens' group, and several became active on the executive and later spoke at the hearings. The group would volunteer to stuff envelopes when information was being mailed to the five hundred plus membership of WDCCG. They were also of the age where participation in protest and peace marches held in Saskatoon was an attraction. This participation was frowned upon by the older folk. I was called upon to explain to a senior why I was allowing the youth to march! I'm sure he was speaking for others as well as himself. While I also had my reservations, I wouldn't veto the young people's plans, although they did understand my reluctance to join them. I was informed by some of the parents that I was spending too much time with this group and leading them in directions the parents weren't comfortable with. I responded by saying that I had a hard time keeping up with them; they were leading me! In retrospect, what was happening was amazing. So many pastors have to plead for people to get involved in projects. Here was a group at the forefront of a movement. A pastor's dream! This group was the church of the present as well as the future. Visit Osler and other area churches today and you'll see that these young adults, now many parents and grandparents, are still making their contribution to church and society.

In the spring of 1979, I realized that the next year would be very intense. The tension in the church was growing, though the leadership was supportive. I decided to offer my resignation as pastor, hoping to alleviate the tension. I believe my resignation was accepted with regret by most of the people. I had completed two out of the three years of the second term for a total of five years. We needed to stay in the community for the next year and within that time would decide on future employment. We were hoping to find employment in the area, for we had found a home there. Our children had their friends and were settled in school. We didn't want to uproot them again. Rhonda was already in her third school. The next year would have many challenges, but as of July 1979, my role as pastor ended. We remained in the congregation for the next twelve months.

It was during the last month as pastor that I experienced doubt, as I wondered if I had made much of a contribution to the church. On one of the last weeks, I decided to stop by for one more visit with a recently widowed member of Osler Mennonite. I didn't really feel like it, but I did it. I was warmly received, and we had a good visit and a little lunch. As I was exiting, she called me back and said she had one more thing to tell me. She said, "Do you remember the Jubilee meeting we had several years ago?" Indeed I did. In March 1975, my first spring there, we had the month set aside to explore biblical themes of social justice as had been outlined by John Howard Yoder in his book, Politics of Jesus. The themes included the forgiveness of debts, the release of slaves, and the return of property lost over the past fifty years. The fiftieth year was the Year of Jubilee! Yoder suggested that Jesus was alluding to these texts as he began his ministry. The themes were introduced in morning worship for four successive weeks and then people would meet in homes in the evening to further discuss the implications for our lives. We had several inter-generational groups meeting. The seniors had no wish to travel out of the village at night, and it was still winter. They proposed to meet as seniors in the village, and Mr. Neudorf would lead them. I wondered how the group would deal with this kind of subject. My hopes were not high. And now, this widow mentioned this event.

She told me that her husband had come home one evening from their study and asked about the forgiveness of debt and what it meant. She explained her understanding, but he interrupted her and said, "What does it mean for me?" Within a few days, he was poring over old financial ledgers. He had been a well-to-do farmer and often had done custom threshing for neighbours. Some had never paid him, and their debts were still listed in his ledger. He took a ruler and pen-stroked out these lines and wrote in, "Forgiven!" It was only a month or two after he had done this that one of the farmers with a debt stopped at his door, wanting to finally pay him what they had owed for several decades. He told the farmer that there was no debt, but the farmer persisted, telling him they had been poor those years but things had improved. Having always felt guilty, he finally wanted to pay what he owed William. William showed them his ledger and the word "Forgiven!" What a story! And I nearly missed it! I would never have expected such an outcome from those lessons. From within the group of seniors, whom I had more or less dismissed, there was a major lesson for me! This came at a time when I needed some reassurance. I have told this story on numerous occasions. A few years ago we were going to Osler to visit our children, and I made arrangements ahead of time to share this story. William's son and daughter-in-law were in attendance. His son was aware of his father's deed and told me it had been a sizable debt.

Life goes on. We make our contributions as well as our many mistakes. We resolve conflict and we create conflict. Our true friends overlook our failings and remain true. Osler was a special place. I have stated that one always remembers one's first love and one's first pastoral position. Rhonda and John, our children, have settled in the community, so we have lots of occasion to go back for a visit. We walk through the community cemetery and take note of recently erected as well as much older headstones. Each has a story of its own. It takes a long time to make that stroll. So many memories. I return to the town, no longer a village, with a clear conscience. And we are always most warmly received!

From Osler to Swift Current

The transition year (1979–80) was a busy and rather difficult one. We needed to get by without a regular paycheque. Judy and I took on a school bus route, and I was able to get many days of employment as harvest labour and, in spring, seeding the next year. Irvin, Wilf, and Ben operated a big farm and always had work for me! Several others would hire me for a day or two. We needed to vacate the parsonage and ended up buying a house on a farmyard with the promise to move the house the next summer. There were no houses available for rent in the area. For the next ten months we lived on the yard with the Giesbrecht family, who were dairy farmers. They had six children, and we had four. Our school bus picked up the eight who were of school age. The biggest stop on the route! We all got along well. I took two courses each semester at the Lutheran seminary in Saskatoon. Our hope was to find an acreage in the area, move our house, establish a yard, and find employment in the area by the next summer.

Meanwhile, a major focus that fall was to prepare for the refinery hearings that were scheduled for three weeks in January 1980. We were a local group of volunteers with no funding, up against a crown corporation with full government backing. No doubt we had worries, yet we had confidence that we represented the local community. The hearings were held during some bitterly cold days. The cold, stormy days did not deter attendance.

The decision reached by the panel wouldn't be released until the following August. By that time, we as a family had relocated to Swift Current. David Ortis, the principal, had recruited me to teach in the area of church history and peace studies at Swift Current Bible Institute. SCBI was a church school for post high school age students. I was quite familiar with all the staff and faculty at the school, since I had been a board member for several years. However, I was a pastor, not a teacher. It would take some adjustment. In preaching, one researches a theme and then condenses it into a twenty-minute sermon. In teaching, one researches a subject and extends it to forty or more lectures! I had realized that my pastoral options in Saskatchewan were slim or nil. My role with the refinery had been very public, and it would be unlikely for any Mennonite congregation to call such a political/radical pastor. I had applied for an MCC position, but the position was only available if we moved to Winnipeg. Even though I felt I wasn't qualified enough for the MCC position, it would have been offered to me if not for the location problem.

I was to become a teacher! We moved in early July and managed to buy an acreage six miles south of the city. The house was an older two-and-a-half-storey building that had recently been upgraded and renovated. (It had originally been built in 1916 with cement blocks and was very sturdy. These blocks had been ordered from Ontario and shipped out west by rail in the early 1910s. In our travels over the next decades, we spotted a number of other houses/buildings erected with the same style of block!) The property was expensive, but we managed to get a mortgage. We also sold eighty acres of our farmland to Harvey, Judy's brother. He had been renting all our farmland since 1973. This allowed us to pay off the mortgage on the farm property in Manitoba, pay back the deposit on the acreage that we had borrowed from my dad, and keep a bit for some repair that still needed to be done.

The house met with the approval of our children. They picked out their bedrooms and explored the five-acre property. Within a week, we took two of the kids to the emergency department of the local hospital. One had stepped on a board with a nail, and the other got a finger mangled by the lawn mower. When asked for our address and family doctor, we had to confess to our recent move and explain that a mailbox and telephone number weren't yet available. The nurses must have wondered what kind of accident-prone family had moved to their city! I vowed that if there was another accident, I would drive the victim to the Herbert hospital, thirty minutes past Swift Current! Fortunately, no more mishaps occurred, and the injured kids quickly recovered.

The yard provided several options. There was lawn around the house, some open grassed areas, and a treed area that would become a pasture. We tilled up a large, grassy area for a market garden. We would establish raspberry and strawberry plots and have lots of room for potatoes, corn, and other garden vegetables. We had plans to market through the farmers' market the next summer. The following spring, we were offered a trampoline by our Uncle John. It was selling at a discount for $735.00. The plan had been to buy a riding mower for the big lawn. We couldn't afford both, so I offered the kids a deal. If they would hand-mow the lawn as long as they were at home, we would buy the trampoline. The offer was quickly accepted. The next summers, they'd divide the lawn in three sections, and each mowed their section on a rotating basis. Swift Current is dry country, so after the middle of July, it didn't take much mowing! The trampoline provided much exercise and enjoyment for our kids and visiting friends. We have now replaced the tarp several times, but the metal structure is secure. It had been a demonstrator when it was built but proved to be too heavy, so only one of that style was ever built. It moved with us to the next three locations and is now used by our grandchildren on our new acreage at Creekside!

On the Swift Current acreage, sheep, goats, calves, cats, and dogs became part of our life. The barn and fences were built to accommodate these creatures. The dog had pups (we were told she had been spayed), the cat had kittens, the sheep had lambs, and the goat had kids—quadruplets! Only the calves had no offspring. There was lots of life in the house and in the barnyard. We recycled where we could. In the fall, we'd haul the corn stalks into the pasture for the sheep to eat. In the spring, we'd spread the manure from the barn in the garden to grow more corn. We'd eat the corn and sell the excess produced. Stalks again went to the sheep! One time, as Michelle was helping with the manure and I was explaining the cycle, she commented, "Wouldn't it be simpler just to eat the manure?" We somehow retained a sense of humour.

The first fall we scattered our different ways. Our two girls were in junior high, Duane was in elementary school, and Jason would start attending kindergarten in the mornings. They would all get on the bus in the morning, and Judy would pick Jason up at noon. She remained a stay-at-home mom till 1986. She was likely the busiest of us all—the quarterback keeping everyone involved and relatively happy. And the chauffeur for after-school events and youth gatherings. The car was always on the go. Lucky for me, I had an old red Datsun quarter-ton truck! Things became easier when Rhonda got her driver's licence.

I was off to SCBI and testing new challenges. I would be teaching three courses each semester the first year and developing the lesson plans as the weeks progressed. I'd come home for supper, have a brief nap after eating, then prepare for the next day's classes. I really spent little time with the family. My involvement likely went down to 5 per cent of the parenting. Fortunately, the long break over the summer helped to make up for some of the lost time. This schedule was repeated for the six years I was teaching. My work became somewhat easier over time but just as busy.

The kids were growing up and graduating from high school. That meant leaving home. Children require the development of roots and wings for healthy living. I believe that was being achieved those years on our acreage! Parents can take some credit, but much growth can take place in spite of parents!

Home life and my teaching life were not as intertwined as they had been at Osler, but they weren't totally separate either. A group of students always responded positively to a home-cooked meal. Residence meals were delicious, but! Some of them marvelled at the goats' milk. One or two offered to do chores if we needed to be away for a while. Also, for special events, the school invited the families of faculty to attend. Orientation of new students could be fun. One fall, all the first-year students were brought into a space occupied by the faculty, staff, and spouses. The students were challenged to match up couples they thought belonged together. There were interesting matches and provided a lot of fun. There were many events like that over the years.

SCBI was set up as a two-year program. The school was founded in 1936 and was designed to train the students in church related positions such as Sunday school teachers, music leaders, and other church leadership responsibilities. Mennonite communities were mainly rural at this time and were fairly isolated from the surrounding society. Most were people who had come to Canada in the 1920s, fleeing the violence experienced in the southern Ukraine. Their main desire was to survive. The preservation of Mennonite faith was also a high priority. These schools, as there were also Bible schools in other provinces, were built to facilitate these desires. By the 1980s much had changed. The churches supporting the school were no longer isolated from the rest of society. While farming was still a major occupation, people had branched out into all areas of life. Higher education had been promoted—not only in church colleges, but in universities as well. SCBI's mandate had changed. The school offered an opportunity for students to discern their path in life. For some, the years there ended their formal education; for others, the years there opened up a wide range of education and future employment opportunities. It was also a place to experience community. Lifelong friendships were created. For some, their friend became their spouse, hence the charge by some that these were "bridal" schools! The students were eighteen to twenty years old, so it was just natural to be considering future marital partners. What better place to date?

I enjoyed working with the faculty and staff at the school. We became friends, not just co-workers. We had a common understanding as to the goals we had for the school. Our educational training had been in Mennonite colleges and seminary, so we were united by an understanding of Anabaptist history and theology, and this formed the basis of the teaching of the school. While some faculty would stay for several years, there was also continual turnover. The school was considered a good place to begin one's employment after training and to discern gifts and interests. Often staff members were single, and married faculty would generally stay for a longer term. When I check the yearbooks from 1980 to 1986, I noted that only two staff members I started with in 1980 were there when I finished in 1986, and one of those had been on a two-year study leave during those six years.

I was one of the married faculty with a teenage family. Salaries weren't high, and budgets were always under stress. The school relied on student tuition and financial support from churches and individuals. We were basically employed for nine months of the year, but our salary could be spread over twelve months. Some faculty survived with spouses who were nurses, teachers, or other vocations. We survived with the rental income we received from our farm in Manitoba. These six years were likely the years of our highest household costs and our lowest salary! We had a mortgage on our acreage, and interest rates were 15 to 18 per cent. Almost all of the monthly payments went to interest, so the principal amount decreased very little. The provincial government did subsidize interest rates that were above 13 per cent. I recall one SCBI board meeting when I was a faculty rep. In the morning, the board approved a sizable increase in salaries. By the afternoon, that decision was reversed when they realized the budget couldn't be balanced. I believe our family financial net worth likely declined during those years. It was the security of our farmland that allowed us to face the future … thanks to that college president, who in 1971 told me not to sell the farm!

Being a two-year program, recruitment of students was ongoing. Most students came from Saskatchewan and Alberta. We also always had some from British Columbia, Manitoba, and occasionally from Ontario. One summer a young man from Ontario came out west after high school to travel and seek work. He ended up on a dairy farm near Osler and accompanied the family to church on Sunday. That's when I met Paul. His family belonged to the United Church back in Ontario and were sheep farmers! By fall, he had decided to attend SCBI, since he had made friends with others who had attended or were students. When he informed his father about his decision, his father wrote him a long letter warning him of the conservative, fundamentalist nature of prairie Bible schools, which might persuade him that the United Church was not a legitimate Christian church. Paul showed me the letter, and I wrote back to his father, telling him that I was aware of the type of schools he was describing but that SCBI was not of that type. We had a respect for the diversity of religious traditions and weren't about "converting" students to our brand (or something like that). Paul would graduate two years later. Then his sister also attended while I was on staff. Her parents came for her grad. Later, a younger brother attended as well. The sister went on to further theological training and became a pastor in a Mennonite congregation in Alberta!

While the majority of our students came from our Mennonite churches, there was considerable diversity as well. A young couple spent two years with us before entering college for further training. They were supported by the Regina Mennonite Church and had come to Canada as "boat people" from Laos. They were learning English as well as coping with their studies in this setting that was very foreign to them. Judy spent a lot of time helping them with their written work. They became family friends and cooked some delicious Laotian meals for us in our home. Some years later, after completing college studies, they returned to Laos as mission workers under the umbrella of the Mennonite Church.

One year, we had several students from the Siksika Nation in Alberta. Among them was a young man who was said to be only sixteen years old. We were asked if we would admit him, as he had been encouraged to attend. Later, we found out he was only fifteen! He attended classes regularly but struggled with academic work. What he did do was hang around with the faculty, listening in on our conversation during coffee breaks. He was very perceptive and was learning in his own style. He voiced a determination to integrate the Christian faith with his community spirituality. This did not meet with the total approval of some of the people who were financially supporting him back in Alberta. He graduated after two years at SCBI. Fortunately, the school didn't have stringent graduation requirements that wouldn't measure the learning that was taking place. (I was academic dean for the last two years and appreciated this aspect!) Decades later, Judy and I were touring the Glenbow Museum in Calgary when we encountered a display of Indigenous history of the Blackfoot people. Herman Yellow Old Woman was listed as a major contributor. Recently, this grad from SCBI was awarded the Alberta 2020 Lieutenant Governor's award for championing the rights of indigenous communities. He was instrumental in the repatriation of a set of regalia that belonged to Chief Crowfoot. These articles had been removed from Canada over a century ago and were displayed in the Royal Albert Museum in Exeter, England. Herman participated in a pipe ceremony in England when the regalia was returned to the Siksika Nation. If SCBI had a distinguished alumni award, I would nominate Herman!

Then there was a young man from a farming family in Saskatchewan who was on the quiet side in class. When he encountered the work of the Mennonite Central Committee in the context of a class, he told himself that this was something he could dedicate his life to. Today, thirty-five years later, Mark is an administrator of international relief work under MCC! Just a few examples of a range of students who roamed the halls of SCBI for a few years. One could never measure the total impact, and many stories would not be widely known.

My final two years at the school were difficult. Everything within the school was going well, but there was unrest in the constituency. There had always been criticism of some nature toward the school. Usually it was in regard to discipline. The school wasn't strict enough in monitoring the behaviour of students. Some should have been expelled, it was stated! But this unrest was different. A group of pastors in the Conference had gathered together and challenged the doctrinal integrity of the faculty. At one point, we were challenged to sign doctrinal statements. We declined to engage in this type of exercise. These pastors had received their training in non-denominational Bible colleges and had little knowledge or appreciation of Anabaptist theology. This is what I consider to be a weakness in the Mennonite church system. Congregations are considered to be independent. There is no "pope" presiding over the churches, so congregations are free to call pastoral leadership from diverse backgrounds. This can be positive if seen as a healthy influx of new thought, but it's dangerous when these pastors believe their mandate is to remake the congregation (and the Conference) to their own liking. Congregations didn't always know what was happening to them. Some would leave the Conference networks entirely and become totally independent.

In our situation as faculty, we felt we were left on our own. I believe we had the support of our board and of the Conference leadership, but these bodies didn't mount a defence on our behalf. The result was that in 1986, there was close to a mass resignation and turnover of staff. I was among those who were tired of the conflict. New staff were hired, and the next school year was underway. I had a bit of a chuckle when I noticed one of the recruited male faculty was wearing an earring! He was a great guy, but the ring must have raised some eyebrows in the constituency.

I vividly recall the next year's provincial conference that was held in the church in Swift Current. We had remained living there, and I had been appointed to the hosting committee for out-of-town delegates. During question time following the SCBI report, a delegate, who was part of the group questioning our integrity, came to the floor and gave his analysis. I thought it strange, for he had never visited the school or talked to any of us in the past six years. His voice was that of authority and sincerity. He felt that the school had "turned the corner." Adjustments had been made, and it was now on the right path. The errors of previous teachings had been removed, and the new faculty looked promising. I was sitting in the balcony listening to all this. Also in the balcony were several SCBI students, now in their second year. I had been one of their teachers. I wondered what they were thinking. The people in Conference leadership were my friends and knew the departed faculty well. Not a word was spoken in our defence. Not one word of challenge! I was devastated and shocked. I believe at that point I resolved to leave church work. I would need to lick my wounds for a long time.

I'm suspicious that I was one of the targets of the opposition. There were people in the Saskatoon area who never thought that my opposition to a uranium refinery was a legitimate faith concern. I'm not sure of their thinking. Were they in favour of uranium and nuclear development? Were they in opposition to the questioning of government policy? Did they believe people of faith had no business in shaping human life on this earth? Did they believe narrowly that the church's responsibility was solely to guide people to appease and submit to a vengeful "God" who would condemn them to hell if they didn't follow a very narrow understanding of the scriptures? Many books have been written exploring the nature of conservative fundamentalism that maintained that there was a pure doctrine. I won't say any more, other than to state that we as faculty experienced some of their wrath. The issues and dynamic were complicated. This has been a difficult and troubling paragraph to write. The next few years will be more pleasant to reflect upon.

We chose to remain in the Swift Current area for the foreseeable future.

Life on the acreage had carried on during the turbulent years. Rhonda had graduated from high school and departed to Winnipeg engaged in MCC's SALT program (Serving and Learning Together). I believe we kept her goats that she'd tended for the past four years. She would meet John in Winnipeg, and eventually they settled as life partners. The wedding took place in Swift Current. Michelle followed her to Winnipeg a year later. Upon graduation, she entered SALT as well and then remained in Winnipeg for further studies. Duane was in high school, following his father's pattern of studying just enough to pass. He completed Grade Twelve and graduated while working part time in an electronics shop to support his lifestyle. He bought his first car at the age of sixteen and his first house a few years later. Jason remained with us and picked a lot of raspberries in the summers to earn money to upgrade his computer equipment. He was entering the electronic age that was foreign to us as parents.

In August of 1986, Judy secured a job in the restaurant business. We were without a regular pay cheque, so she offered to work while I looked for some work on a harvest crew, as we were surrounded by wheat fields. The first morning I set out to see if work was available. The first farmer had sufficient help. The second hired me on the spot. I was so fortunate that Ken hired me. The next neighbour down the road would have been very difficult to work for. I didn't realize that at the time, but I heard the stories! These stories were confirmed when I helped him haul some grain the next winter.

Later that fall, I applied for a term position to teach in the Cypress Hills Community College. The college was advertising for an instructor in job readiness training. Meanwhile, Judy didn't see much future waiting on tables (even though her boss told her that he would never fire her), so we were testing the possibilities of establishing a consignment store for children's clothing. It was a busy fall. I secured the college position that would start in January. We found a storefront to rent, and I started building racks for clothing, tables, and counters. We painted these in bright colours. It took some time before we could register our chosen name: Encore Children's Wear. Advertising and promotion followed, and this new venture opened early the next year.

Meanwhile, Judy and I planned a brief trip. We booked tickets on VIA to travel through the Rockies to the west coast. Jason and a friend of his would come as well. His friend's grandparents lived in the Fraser Valley and were prepared to host the boys for the week we were there. Judy and I visited with friends and toured the city of Vancouver as well as Vancouver Island. We experienced winter … or the lack of winter … and were astonished as to how green the places were. Soon it was time to head back home. The train travel was a big attraction of this trip. We had sleeping accommodation and ate meals in the dining car. The dome seats offered all the mountain views one could wish for. Really, the best trip to take is truly by rail!

Back to reality in Swift Current. Judy prepared Encore for its opening, and I was back in the classroom. There were just over twenty participants in the class. They ranged in age from late teens to over fifty. They were mostly female with just two male students. The course was designed to prepare these clients for the workplace. Their tuition and living costs were covered while they participated in this government initiative. Building up self confidence was a major goal. Some had experienced marital failure and needed a job to support themselves if they wished to get off social assistance. It was a new experience for me and a new glimpse into this segment of society. Unemployment rates were around 10 per cent in the province.

The class was a six-hour seminar, five days a week, for close to six months. Again, I felt lacking in qualifications but was getting used to it! These were adults who had considerable life experience. There could be no pretending. Teaching clear communication styles was important. I recall one of the male students recounting a conversation he'd had with a neighbour the evening before, saying, "He has absolutely no communication skills!" Here was a person who had just recently learned these skills in the past month! Another student, a mother with three children living on social assistance, stated that she could only take one day at a time. That was her coping strategy. I heard what she was saying and then gently spoke about the need to plan ahead as well. She needed to make some plans beyond the next day to get out of the dilemma she was in. Partway through the course, one of the women with a young family received a job offer in Alberta and accepted it. A big step. Rather devastating for one of the males, for he had his eye on her, and it appeared the relationship was progressing. All kinds of things going on!

The college provided strong support for its staff. Evaluation was ongoing, which I valued since I was so new to this kind of setting. At one point, I told my supervisor that I was unsure of how I was doing. He asked me how many students had quit the course. When I told him that none had quit, he said I was doing fine. He said these adult students wouldn't tolerate inadequate instruction. They'd be gone. It was reassuring to hear that. My salary was also a surprise! I was given credit for my six years of teaching experience at SCBI and was on the provincial teachers' salary scale! That scale was considerably higher than the church scales!

The last weeks of class involved preparing the students for job interviews. We had covered the different aspect of this experience. How to dress. Should one ask questions? Being honest about past employment. How to state one's qualifications, inquiring what the salary would be, etc. We then conducted mock interviews. I asked them to choose a job they wanted to apply for, and then I would conduct the interview in a formal way. A few other students could observe this session and offer feedback later. This worked rather well. The students were ready to face the world, Some for the second or third time.

Summer came and the classes were over. The garden had been planted in the meanwhile and needed to be weeded. I was asked to come back to the college for two weeks in July to work with the same group of clients. They were to write out their resumes and arrange for interviews in actual jobs that were being posted. They would come to class and then would scatter into the community doing their job search. Several were able to secure employment, and all gained experience. It was interesting to have them relate how closely their training was reflected in their actual experience (or not!). When I asked a young fellow how his interview had gone for a position in a garage, he told me it was conducted outside with the boss hanging out the window of his truck! Not quite the formal process he had been expecting!

This had been a term position, and there was no guarantee that another term would be available for the next year. I was made aware of a position being offered by the Neil Squire Foundation based in Vancouver. It was for a three-year pilot project to be conducted at the college in Swift Current. The position would be to assist severely physically disabled adults to become comfortable with the use of computers. Awareness of computer technology was required as well as some experience working with people who were physically disabled. I had taken a computer awareness short course as required for my previous employment. Computers were just starting to have an impact on employment. I also visited with a friend who was an occupational therapist. I wanted to learn more about being severely physically disabled. Causes, I was told, ranged from accidents causing spinal cord injuries to a range of diseases such as arthritis, MS, ALS, and being born with cerebral palsy. I was ready for the interview to be conducted in Regina. I had practised with the college students, so I should be prepared!

In late November, I received a letter stating that I was hired and would start work in December. An early Christmas gift! The position would be for two-and-a-half years, which was the time remaining in the three-year pilot project. Finally, a bit of employment stability! The main project for the NSF was based in Vancouver and funded by a multi-million-dollar federal grant. The grant required one site in a city other than Vancouver (Regina) as well as a site in a rural setting, which would be Swift Current. Neil Squire, after whom the foundation was named, was a young man who'd had a serious skiing accident. He became a quadriplegic, unable to move any parts of his body below his neck. His uncle, Bill Cameron, an engineer, would visit Neil in the hospital where Neil would likely have to spend the rest of his life. Bill was dismayed with the severe limitations to Neil's future and began to experiment with creating computer applications that Neil could use. He designed a "sip and puff" system that would enable Neil to bypass the keyboard. Letters of the alphabet were lined up by combinations of sipping and puffing with one's breath! It was slow going, but it worked! Bill went on to further develop this system, and later the NSF was born. The long-range goal was to create a path for adults with severe physical disabilities to access the workplace and become more independent and even become taxpayers.

I was starting from scratch in Swift Current, but I had strong support from my immediate supervisor in Regina, and we remained in close contact throughout the years. My introduction was to attend a disabled farmers' conference in Regina. Attending was a young farmer from Crystal City who had lost a leg in a farming accident. He wasn't a candidate for our computer training, since he wasn't considered severely disabled within our mandate. I mention him here just to indicate how small the world is at times! He went on to win an Olympic gold medal in wheelchair curling in Sochi, Russia! While at the conference, I was introduced to Arnold, a university student who was to demonstrate his computer skills to the farmers. He used a stick in his mouth with which he accessed the computer keyboard. What people didn't realize was that he didn't just do word processing—he was a programmer! He had cerebral palsy and motored his wheelchair by pushing with his feet, which propelled him backward! Rhonda had met him at the university in Saskatoon. He, along with our staff, ordered fast food for supper. Arnold ordered a massive burger with all the trimmings. When the food was delivered, he and I were left on our own. I looked at my burger and then at his. I knew how I would eat mine, but Arnold had no use of his hands. I asked him how he would eat his burger. He said, with his slurred words, "Same as yours! With your hands!" So I proceeded to pick up his burger and shove it toward his mouth, and he'd take the biggest bite he could, with mustard and ketchup dripping down his chin. Later, when my supervisor reappeared, I told her of my supper experience and felt I shouldn't have been left on my own. This was my second or third day on the job! She laughed and said Arnold is good for all of us!

I was learning how the Swift Current project was to proceed. I was in charge and would have a "computer comfort" instructor on site. This instructor was a University of Regina student who was on a four-month work term relating to his field of study. I was to identify potential clients in our part of the province who might benefit from this instruction. My co-worker would then work one-to-one with these clients, who had likely never faced a computer screen before. Thus, "computer comfort!" Having up-to-date computers was a problem. A computer company had granted over a hundred of their obsolete computers to the NSF, and we got several of these that were very difficult to operate. When we received some IBM compatible models later on, they were well received.

A rancher in the southwest of our area was identified as a possible participant in our program. He had a high spinal cord injury as the result of being bucked off a horse. He had limited use of one arm and some control of a few fingers. He was to secure housing in Regina after his lengthy stay in the hospital, where he would be in an assisted-living setting. But he was a rancher and insisted on moving back to his home where he would receive care from his mother and sister. Because his caregivers were family, he was disqualified from government assistance! This policy was being challenged at the time. We paid him a visit and offered him one of our obsolete computers and some instruction. He was reluctant to try much for the first while. He lived over an hour's distance from our office, so we couldn't go out that often. After some time, we brought him a newer model to try. He was immediately impressed as he used his one finger on the keyboard. He had a close neighbour who was often there with us and was hoping against hope that his friend would accept this new technology. The neighbour gave me the thumbs up signal. We had our new client hooked!

Some time later, two of the Vancouver staff were visiting "the rural project" and wanted to see this rancher. I drove them out, taking the usual route and some shortcuts I'd used before. Within a few miles of the ranch, we encountered water running over a dip in the road. To turn back would take another hour, so I got out and found a stick to measure the depth of the water. It wasn't that deep, and I couldn't see any washout of the road. It was maybe ten to twelve feet across, and I said we could make it. This would give these two young women from Vancouver something to talk about when they got home! We made it! At the ranch, the former rancher displayed some of his new skills. Apparently, he was tracking the financial markets and trading stocks for some of his neighbours, who told him he was making more money for them than their cows were!

We discovered that there were no people in the rural area with the most severe disabilities that would require the sip and puff method. These people needed to remain in the cities because of the level of support they required. A junior hockey player playing for the Regina Pats suffered a devastating injury during these years. I remember meeting him a few months later in the hospital. His injury was similar to Neil Squire's. In the coming years, technology advanced, and this young former hockey player benefited from these changes. Imagine my surprise twenty-five years later when I read a newspaper article that told of his story and that he was employed as a scout for the Regina Pats. He had a remarkable ability to identify hockey talent, all from his wheelchair and his computer with no movement of his body from his neck down. A fulfillment of Bill Cameron's dream!

Time was running out and the funding of the pilot project was coming to a close. What would we do next? I had recovered somewhat from the SCBI pain and realized that I still had the training for pastoral ministry. Should I test out this option again? At some point we did test it with a congregation in Brandon, but the process of that congregation was flawed, and they ended up courting several prospects at the same time. We didn't make the cut, and the other candidate withdrew his application. The congregation had to start over again! After that experience, Judy and I decided to stay on our acreage. We had friends in the area and were appreciating our involvement in Jubilee Mennonite Fellowship. This was a newer congregation that had formed in the area a few years earlier. Jason was entering high school, and Duane had employment and was living at home at the time. The only major issue was my employment. Encore was experiencing considerable traffic and providing a good service to the community but would never support us financially.

Then one evening the phone rang and everything changed!

Back to Manitoba, Springstein

We had made the decision to remain at Swift Current, but there was the nagging problem of my employment. The short-term jobs I'd held over the past three years weren't ideal, and to find a more permanent position would be difficult without further training. When the phone rang that evening, Judy answered it, and after a minute or two gave the phone to me. "It's Ron Loeppky," she told me. "He wants to talk about a pastoral position." Ron was a former acquaintance from Manitoba. I took the phone and went into another room. Almost an hour later, Judy came into my room, wondering why I was still talking to him. After all, we had decided not to move. Ron had convinced me that he was serious with his invitation for us to consider a pastoral position in the Springstein Mennonite Church close to Winnipeg. He had checked around with people who knew me better, inquiring about my suitability for their congregation. He'd be coming to Saskatoon in a few weeks and wondered if we could meet him there over supper. It had taken some convincing on his part. I warned him about my reputation! Finally, I agreed to at least talk. We arranged a date and place that would be suitable. That meeting took place, and after much discussion, we agreed to visit the congregation for a weekend in March 1990.

The coming year was shaping up to be pretty busy. We would be travelling to Manitoba to scout out this church. If it was an option, it would require more trips and then the major move. We would need to sell our acreage. We were planning to celebrate our twenty-fifth wedding anniversary on our yard with our parents, siblings, and their families, and we had made arrangements to attend the Mennonite World Conference in Winnipeg in July! Then we heard that Ray (my nephew) and Karen were planning a wedding. Regrettably, we had to inform them that we wouldn't be able to come.

We decided to take a short trip in January to celebrate our anniversary, since there would be no time later that year. We took a road trip through northern Montana, crossing the border in the remote southwest corner of Saskatchewan. We encountered "Texas gates" just across the border. These were designed to keep cattle in the pastures while still allowing traffic through on the highway. We wandered west and crossed mountain ranges into Idaho. It was winter, and we experienced snowstorms in the higher elevations and then rain in the valleys. I recall the "Pie Place" establishments, with dozens of assorted pies, and the viewing of the movie *Parenthood*, featuring Steve Martin. The movie was comical as well as sobering. It revealed to us that parenting never really ends. We had thought our role as parents was almost complete! We crossed into British Columbia and were stranded overnight due to highways blocked by snow. We did make it home after watching a Flames hockey game in Calgary!

We were now ready to face the rest of the year. Judy went back to Encore, and I continued with the Neil Squire Foundation. The trip to Springstein in March was meant to be a low-key affair to give us a feel for the congregation and meet some of the people. On Sunday morning, we sat with the congregation in their worship service. Two meetings had been arranged, and I learned about their expectations of leadership. I spoke about my "style" and what I might contribute to their congregation. The weekend was favourable to both parties, so another, more formal visit was planned for the spring. (It was still winter in March. There was much more snow than we had been experiencing out west!)

The next visit was more involved. I was to preach the sermon that Sunday, and the importance of this was downplayed to ease the pressure. In fact, the advice to pastors was not to preach one's best sermon on such an occasion! If you did, the congregation would be disappointed in all the ones to follow!

We got a tour of the rural community and were told about life in the village. We had expressed interest in finding an acreage, but the congregation was insisting that the pastor live in the provided parsonage next to the church. I wondered, following this discussion, if they were looking for a pastor or for renters! Jason was with us on this trip. He would be entering Grade Ten, so we toured the school in Sanford as well as a private Mennonite school in Winnipeg. A few students from the village were attending the private school, so carpooling was an option. Discussion regarding salaries was necessary as was a timeline for final decisions regarding the "call." They would make their decision fairly quickly after our visit, and then we could respond. It wasn't long and our future was determined. We'd move in late September, and I would start my position in November.

The move took place in stages. We took a vanload of possessions to Manitoba in early September, and we were also moving Jason and his cat. He would be living in Winnipeg with his sister, Michelle, and attending Westgate Mennonite Collegiate. We followed a month later with a large U-Haul van loaded to the top with the remaining household goods. Friends helped us load that morning as we had helped others move over the past few years. Our acreage had not been sold. The economy was poor, and real estate, especially acreages, was not easily sold. We did have a young couple interested, but they needed to sell their house in Swift Current before they could buy our property. This didn't happen until the next spring. I went back to Swift Current one more time that fall to load our Datsun truck with yard and farm items. I had thought there wasn't much left but ended up overloaded! I was stopped by the RCMP somewhere in eastern Saskatchewan, who wanted to check my overloaded truck. I assured them that everything was in order, and I made it back to Springstein with no problem. Our move was now complete.

The congregation was a lively one. All age groups were represented, and people were eager to engage in discussion on a full range of topics. Outwardly, it appeared that people had their lives in order. I soon discovered, however, that this group of people was like all others. Congregation members were dealing with all kinds of issues within their family lives. Some past conflicts in the community had never been adequately resolved. Some went back generations. In the four rural congregations I spent time in, there wasn't one where I didn't discover a conflict arising from a land transaction between congregation members. These had all happened decades ago but hadn't been resolved in a satisfactory manner. Some parents were upset with their children's decisions, etc. Like I said, it was a normal congregation. There were many opportunities to provide pastoral care.

The congregation had completed a major building project the previous decade to accommodate the growth that was being experienced. In 1988, the church celebrated their fiftieth anniversary with a massive celebration. Two years later, they were still talking about it! There was pride in their voices, and rightfully so. I was installed as their pastor in early December. This event called for a "recitation" of the church's history and tradition. The list of impressive former leaders was detailed, and their contributions noted. Expectations were high, it seemed to me. Among Mennonite churches, Springstein could be considered "high church," if one uses a Lutheran or Anglican term. This speaks of order and formality. I later came to understand this more as the view of the senior members. The younger generation was more casual in their approach. But up on the platform, waiting to be installed, I felt inadequate to meet their expectations. There was no backing out now. Both sets of parents and other relatives were in attendance. It would have been a scandal for me to decline the installation! It didn't really enter my mind to do that, but I wondered how I would fit into their roster of former pastors. Some time later, I mentioned to the leader that morning what had gone through my mind. He apologized, stating that he might have gotten carried away!

It wasn't long until I was fully engaged in this new setting. There were many committees, and I was determined to attend all the meetings. I should have known better! I was told it wasn't necessary for me to be at all of them, but no one told me which ones to miss. I also was determined to get to know all the members personally. The directory of families had been updated recently, and Judy and I both studied it thoroughly to memorize names. People were impressed how quickly we were able to do this. I'd had lots of practice at SCBI with a new group of students every fall! I also consulted the membership and family records to find out who was related to whom. There were several large extended family networks that I needed to sort out. One time, a few years later, I referred to two people who were seniors and were brother and sister to one another. I was challenged that this wasn't correct by someone who had lived there all his life, but I persisted in my view. Later, he acknowledged that I was correct and said that he now understood why these two couples often travelled together for holidays! He thought they were just very good friends. He never guessed that they might be related!

There were a number of widows in the congregation living in Winnipeg, either in their own homes or in an apartment. They were rarely able to come to the services in Springstein, so my only opportunity to meet them was to visit them in their homes. They had lived their earlier days with their husbands and children on a farm in the country. They still considered themselves members at Springstein, so I was their new pastor. I phoned one of the widows to arrange for a visit. It seemed as if she had been expecting a call. She accepted me readily, for she had a respect for the "office" of minister. She didn't need to know me personally. If the congregation had called me to be their pastor, I must be okay! She was prepared for my visit. She invited me into her living room and showed me where I should sit. We chatted for a while to become acquainted, and then she brought me a Bible to read. "Read a portion," she said, "and then say a prayer!" She knew how pastoral visits were to take place. After the prayer, we had faspa together, and the visit ended.

Quite a different visit was experienced with another widow, although the circumstances were similar. She had moved to Winnipeg after her husband's death. In this visit, I didn't need to worry about carrying the conversation. She switched languages from English to Low German and back again several times! She told me stories of her childhood in South Russia and the years of pioneer life on the Canadian prairies. There had been poverty and a considerable amount of family tragedy. Then she referred to something that had happened last week! When I returned home for supper after the faspa with the widow, I told Judy I was never quite sure what country she was referring to or in which decade the story had taken place. Both these visits were delightful events, despite the total difference. These people had much to share, and I gradually learned more of the history of Springstein and its people!

Judy was rather restless, not sure where to find a new niche. She no longer had her business to run, so she secured a number of volunteer, short-term positions in Winnipeg. Then she was asked to apply for a position at CMBC. While waiting for the decision, she travelled back to Saskatchewan to visit our children. When she came home, I had two surprises for her. She had been offered the position at CMBC, and we had a fifteen-year-old boarder living with us! While she was gone, some dramatic things had happened in our ordinarily quiet neighbourhood. A young boy from Guatemala had made his appearance. He had illegally crossed three international borders to arrive in Manitoba. He had escaped a dangerous situation in his home country and was full of tales of travel and survival. We started the process to secure legal status for him with Canada Immigration, and our family was appointed his guardian. I had met with some folks from the church and was assured of congregational support.

William found a home in our community and was somewhat of a hit due to his infectious smile and demeanour. He enrolled in school with hopes of improving his English. But the coming winter was difficult for him, and without consultation, he left our home early one January morning after having lived with us for eight months. He left by bike, and we believed he headed west. Fortunately, the weather was exceptionally warm with only minor frost at night. I feared for his survival and had alerted the RCMP. They weren't going to do a search for him but did place his name in their data bank in case he showed up somewhere. We never heard from him and have no idea where he might be or if he made it back to Guatemala. Is he dead or alive? His brief note had mentioned his desire to go home.

Another major effort of our church was our involvement with the Jimmy Carter Habitat for Humanity house build in Winnipeg in 1993. Eighteen houses were to be built. I had discovered this project while wondering how to get the men of the congregation involved in a more practical way. I stopped by the Habitat office in Winnipeg seeking information and wondering if we might get involved. That was when I was informed about the 1993 goal of the organization. I asked them if a speaker would be available to come to one of our Sunday worship services to inform us about their work in providing homes for the working poor with interest-free mortgages. That worked out well. The Service Committee of the church accepted this project as a goal for our church, and we also accepted the challenge of raising funds for the build. Our goal was to raise enough funds for one house as well as enlist volunteers for a week of construction the following July. I preached a sermon on Christmas gift giving well before Christmas, challenging the congregation to divert their gifts to Habitat for the coming Christmas. I had calculated how much adults spent on one another (I excluded children) and reasoned with them that it wouldn't cost them any more than normal. Just divert the money spent on a spouse or other adults to this project for this year.

William and Jason 1992

Enough people responded to the challenge so that we raised over $13,000.00 that year! We were not as successful in recruiting people for the construction labour for the summer, but we did have a large crew of fathers and sons gather one Saturday in the winter to do a "pre-build" of floors in a large warehouse. This was under Habitat supervision and was done in preparation for the summer project. A smaller crew joined daily with Jimmy Carter and hundreds of other volunteers in erecting eighteen houses within a week in the summertime! And we had a crew serve some of the meals on site for the hungry workers. I recall them giving our Springstein volunteer carpenters a rousing cheer when we approached the lunch counter! Overall, it was a very successful venture.

There was lively interaction within the congregation as faith and lifestyle issues were being sorted out. The church elected four male deacons who had specific responsibilities for the spiritual life of the members. I met with them regularly. Their spouses joined the group, and one of the deacons raised the issue that the pastor's spouse wasn't attending as the former pastor's wife had done. Judy wasn't that kind of a pastor's spouse, and the issue was resolved with the one deacon who had raised it. This same deacon (a senior member) once showed me a letter he had received from the religious radio broadcast, *Back to the Bible*. He had written to this organization asking about their view of women in leadership in the church. The letter he received stated that it was unbiblical. I asked him why he hadn't written to one of the professors at CMBC. He knew several of them, for they would, on occasion, preach in the church. He looked me in the eye and with a twinkle in his own replied, "Because I knew what they would say!" Case closed. We had our differing views, but it never interfered with our mutual respect for one another. These were the issues of the time, and the congregation was sorting out how to approach the future. It wasn't much later that women were eligible for both deacon and pastor roles.

Often differing views became generational issues. How does one offer some changes as well as respect the tradition? This became an issue with the Maundy Thursday service one year. My first year or two, it was conducted in a traditional way with the serving of communion following the sermon. The next morning, a Good Friday service would be held, followed by the Easter service on Sunday. It was a busy weekend, and this model had been followed for many decades. I heard rumblings after the weekend that some alterations needed to be made to the Maundy Thursday service.

I happened to find a script for a reader's theatre presentation that was well suited for that service. In advance of the next year's service, I pulled the script from my files and shared it with the worship committee. They wholeheartedly approved of it. This committee then relayed the plans to the church council at their next meeting, and there was no objection. Plans were underway. We needed to recruit twelve men to serve as disciples of Jesus. I was to play the Jesus role. There were minimal requirements of the disciples, just a few words to read following the gospel account. I, as Jesus, would speak a few words of affirmation to each disciple in turn. Communion would be served to this group on stage and then to the gathered congregation.

Enough willing men were found. Several were on the fringes of active involvement in worship and likely hadn't had this kind of congregational involvement in playing a role on stage since their Sunday school days! Costumes were provided. The production was gaining momentum and would be better than originally envisioned. Early in the week of this service, I had a call from Bill that there was a concern being voiced among some of the seniors. They were determined to boycott this service. I was told to cancel it! There were three days until the service. I replied that we had gone through all the channels of leadership and had received their approval. I also said that I couldn't disappoint the "disciples" who had agreed to be involved. Besides, there was no alternative plan to replace this service. Bill persisted, however, and warned me that a number of seniors would miss the communion service. It was ironic that these people's sons and sons-in-law would be in the service. I made some calls to council members, and we agreed to go ahead with the service.

The church was almost full, though a certain age group was smaller in number. There was total approval of the service. People in attendance found it very meaningful. One disciple had tears in his eyes at its conclusion! Bill stopped by the office the next week and told me it had been a very good service. I gave him credit for coming even when he disapproved. Maybe he wasn't opposed to the service and had merely reported to me what he was hearing. Then he said, "Don't do it again!" One of the senior women later apologized for not being there. Her son had been one of the disciples. I was relieved when the week was over. It had been an exercise in balancing the call for change with respecting tradition. The congregation was true to form, however. No one held a grudge. I had been told at the time of my hiring that there was a desire for the worship experience to be enhanced. But how to do this and not upset some people? When I told some of the leadership that I had been hired under false pretenses, they responded that I had been doing a lot of enhancing!

I suppose that these experiences were those of conflict management. I wondered how I was doing. I had heard that J.J. Thiessen, who was a former Conference leader for many years as well as the pastor of First Mennonite Church, Saskatoon, had given the following advice to a new pastor: "Listen carefully to both sides. Consider what is being said. Then do the right thing!" Was that helpful? I had asked Walter Franz what it was like to be back in a pastoral role after some time away while he was principal of SCBI. His journey had started in Osler, then a stint at the Bible school, then back as a pastor in Altona, Manitoba. He told me that in his early years when conflict happened, everyone panicked. Later, he had learned to accept that there was conflict and to deal with it! That was helpful.

At a later deacon meeting a conflict was resolved by an unexpected source. The deacons had planned a communion service and set the date. There were specific periods on the church calendar when these services were held, but they could also be planned for other occasions. This was just before summer, if I recall correctly. After the plans were confirmed, someone (not me) suggested that a potluck could follow the service. The congregation was from a fairly wide geographic area, with several families living in Winnipeg. They loved staying for potlucks after church services and catching up on visiting. However, one deacon objected, saying he didn't approve of a noisy gathering after the solemn observance of the Lord's Supper. No one agreed with him, but the discussion went back and forth for some time. He said he wouldn't attend. Then his wife, who had never before voiced her view on any issue, asked her husband, "Where will you have your lunch then?" The issue was resolved! The deacon came to the service, and it was a great Sunday!

I did have a minor conflict with our neighbour (actually with his dog) during our last winter at Springstein. A new family had moved in next door to us, and they had a large dog. There was a lot of snow, and I noticed a build up of dog droppings all over our back lawn. One morning as I was leaving the house to go across the back yard to the church office, the neighbour's door opened, and the dog dashed out to our back lawn and did what I suspected he had been doing for some time. But how to approach this matter? The lawn would be a mess in spring. By the time I came home for lunch, a plan had formulated in my mind. I knocked on the door, and Terry came out. After a word of greeting (I had chatted with him several times, but just short conversations), I said, "Terry, I like you as a neighbour, but I have a bone to pick with your dog!" He asked what the problem was, so I told him. At first, defensively, he asked how I knew it was his dog. I told him that I had observed it and had caught the dog red-handed that morning. He relented and said he'd take care of it! No problem. I was kind of proud that I had figured out a way to place the blame on the dog and not on the neighbour! The next spring, Terry sold us his older F-150 Ford truck with a cap that would be ideal for the venture that awaited us!

Things were changing in our family life. Judy and I became grandparents in the spring of 1992 when Noah was born to John and Rhonda. Jem would be added to their family two years later. The congregation celebrated with us. In June, on a beautiful Saturday, Michelle and Don were married. The wedding was held at Camp Assiniboia, just a few miles north of Springstein. It was an outdoor event, and the weather couldn't have been better. In December I turned fifty! I awoke that morning and noticed something on our lawn. Close to fifty pink, plastic flamingos had been stuck in the snow overnight all over our front lawn, the ditch, and our driveway. Apparently, this "flock" had made previous appearances in the village whenever someone turned fifty! Some must have flown south, since there weren't quite fifty! The year 1993 also held several highlights for our family. In January, Judy and I took a trip to Australia to visit my brother, Dave, and his wife, Romaine. Dave had been in Australia since the early 1970s and had come back home to visit a few times, but this was our first trip to see him. It was a great trip! In June, Jason graduated from high school and would study at CMBC the following year. My initial three-year term was extended for another term after a review process of the first three years was completed. I accepted the renewal and stated, however, that I would start the term but didn't promise to complete the full three years. I think the congregation may have been puzzled by this comment.

For some reason, I was feeling restless. I had kept a "Basic Mood Indicator" log starting in late 1992. Somewhere, I had become aware of this tool to chart one's mood concerning discouragement and even depression. The indicator allowed one to estimate one's mood with eight stages ranging from very low to very high. I recorded it daily for a month and after that made periodic comments assessing how I was feeling. I noted my mood generally as in the plus or minus medium range. There were no lows or highs. I had a boost after our Australia trip, but took a dip due to the issue of facing a review and extension of term in 1993. At that time, I was looking beyond the next three years and wondering how long I would stay in pastoral work. I severely lacked a life/work balance, as I was spending all my time and energy in pastoral work.

I was out of shape physically and didn't find a way of getting into shape. I went biking with a friend one day. Only half a mile along the paved highway, I was out of breath and stated that I needed to turn back! My friend had been a long-distance biker and was surprised at my lack of stamina. For me, it was a bad signal. I did some cross-country skiing in winter and quite a bit of golfing in summer, but it wasn't enough and didn't happen on a regular basis. I was asked to be a substitute curler one evening. I couldn't participate in regular curling, since these were evening schedules and I had a lot of evening meetings. I was severely winded sweeping the rocks that evening! I was my own worst enemy. I was too committed to my pastoral role and not recognizing the impact it was having on my overall health. Due to my poor moods, I needed more affirmation from the congregation than one can expect to receive. I noted in my log that after I accepted the renewal of term, only a few voiced their appreciation to me directly. Most people rightly believed the strong vote in favour of the extension should be affirmation enough.

In the fall of 1993, a lot of things changed. An opportunity came about allowing us to move back to our farm and take a part-time position as pastor in an area congregation. I would be involved in the physical work of construction and then in farming. The longer term future looked brighter. I no longer kept up with the log, unless I came across the file when looking for something else. For many reasons it would be difficult to leave Springstein. We had been a good match. I credit the congregation with being a place of "healing" after my discouragement at Swift Current. This experience allowed me to continue in pastoral work for another eight years until my retirement. At the end of September 1994, we would be busy with the major job of restoring our old farmhouse. Mid-afternoon one day, I was running up the long staircase. Someone had called me for some construction advice. I stopped before I was at the top and laughed! I had already put in many hours of work that day, and I was still running up the stairs. I was in shape after three months of physical work! Amazing! My final entry in the log was on December 5, 1997. I came across the file while looking for Advent resources. My final sentence states, "Life is very different here. One wonders if one could have survived in full-time ministry at Springstein or elsewhere."

One Saturday fall evening, still at Springstein, I was browsing through the *Winnipeg Free Press*. My sermon for the next morning was ready. I had never paid any attention to the want ads, but as I turned a page, an ad on the top corner caught my eye. A used thirty-horsepower diesel tractor was listed for sale, along with more than six other implements. The tractor also had a front-end loader with two different buckets. Plans were in progress to move back to our farm, and this purchase would be an asset to our work there. The next day, Judy and I took the drive thirty miles east of Winnipeg to take a look. It was exactly as advertised. The young man who was showing us the equipment informed us that his father, who had recently passed away, had been the owner. He now wanted to clear out all the items in one sale and was willing to take offers. I took the tractor for a ride and tried out the loader and the attached tiller. Everything was in working order. There had been a price indicated in the ad, but I made a somewhat lower offer and he replied, "Sold!" The next week, I made arrangements with Garry, who had a truck and trailer unit, to go to pick up the purchase. We were able to load everything except the tractor. We considered coming back in a few days to pick it up, but a suitable day wasn't available. I said I would drive it home. I was wearing heavy coveralls but had to borrow a toque from the owner. It was a three-to-four-hour trip, but I made it home for supper! The next week we delivered the trailer load to Crystal City. This was the first step of our move back home. There would be many more trips before our final departure, still eight months in the future.

After we left Springstein, we still had occasional contact with people we had gotten to know. (We always had time for pleasant chats!) While at a garden centre one spring near Headingley, we met one of the couples from the church. While the women chatted and compared purchases, we men were left on our own. The two of us had never had much conversation during our four years at Springstein, but now we talked up a storm. He was genuinely happy to see me! A similar event happened a few years later. We had been invited to the wedding of a young woman, a farrier, who had trimmed the hooves of our horses for several years. We were surprised at the invitation but wouldn't miss it. It was a Catholic wedding in Manitou, and we didn't expect to see any familiar faces other than the bride. Lo and behold, a couple from Springstein showed up. They were friends with the groom's parents. We ended up sitting together with them for the reception. We were the only people there whom they knew, other than the groom's parents. We also talked up a storm. George hadn't always been as faithful as his wife in attending services, and I'd had little opportunity to get to know him. He was a busy farmer and businessman. The first thing he asked me was what my reaction had been when the priest asked the non-Catholics in attendance not to come forward for the communion. I had expected that we would be excluded, but George was rather upset that he was not considered worthy! We had a delightful time. We were happy to meet someone we knew, but more so that I finally got to know him better. He related all the places he had lived and how he had ended up at Springstein. As I considered these two experiences, I realized that for certain men, the pastor was a rather unusual creature and difficult to converse with. What was there in common that would make for casual banter? I was now a former pastor, and barriers had disappeared!

Major Decision Two

I have outlined part one of what I called our two best decisions in a previous chapter. What follows is an accounting of part two of these two best decisions.

In July 1992, Judy and I took two weeks of holidays and camped on our old farmyard at Crystal City. We began the process of gutting the interior of the house that had stood empty for over twenty years. Our daughter Michelle had chided us for allowing our old house to slowly rot away. She told us that there was a lot of good lumber there, but something needed to be done soon. I had no interest in doing anything, stating that it was very difficult to dismantle an old house and save the good trim, baseboards, etc. Most would be ruined in the process. Besides, it was just the nature of abandoned farm buildings. They had been built, served their purpose, and in time replaced by new buildings or left for nature to dismantle. I finally relented and agreed to go out to the farm on the May long weekend to confirm my suspicions. It was a test run. If unsuccessful, we'd forget about trying to do anything with it. If successful, we'd evaluate our options.

We went equipped with some wrecking bars and started in Rhonda's room. It actually went fairly well. We were able to pry off the trim around the windows and doors, as well as the baseboards. We opened up part of the wall by removing a section of the lath and plaster. The studding looked good, and we were able to pull out nails from the fir lumber with normal effort. The test turned out to be positive. That's why we were camping on the yard in July. It was hot and dirty work, but there was satisfaction in doing physical work. We were making progress moving the recovered material and storing it in the barn. We shovelled the lath and plaster out the window and dumped it in the old bank barn site. It was good to clean up as we went along. Some evenings we went in to visit the parents in town (and to take showers), and some evenings were spent around the campfire visiting with friends and cousins who had stopped by to see what we were doing. There was a great deal of curiosity in the community about what we were up to. We were beginning to fall in love with our former home community.

This two-week experience was repeated in July 1993. By the end of that time, almost all of the interior had been gutted, and the barn was full of the stored material. Earlier in June, I had arranged with Garry Daught, pastor at Mather and a friend from Swift Current days, to exchange pulpits the first Sunday of July. He was to conduct the service in Springstein, and I'd take his place in Mather at Trinity Mennonite Fellowship. We also offered the Daught family access to the parsonage at Springstein so that they could explore Winnipeg for a few days. Garry stopped by the farm to make final arrangements a few days before the weekend.

"What are you people doing here?" he asked in amazement. We gave a brief sketch of our plans, explaining that we were dismantling the house and storing the lumber, planning to use it to build a new house if we could find a suitable location close to Winnipeg. "Why don't you rebuild here? This is a beautiful spot!" Wheels were turning in his head, and he asked if we knew he had tendered his resignation at Trinity, effective July 1994. Possibly we could take his place. He asked if he could breathe our name to the search committee. Too much at once! I told him I had just started my second term at SMC, so the timing wasn't good. We talked some more, and I finally consented to allowing him to mention my name to the committee at some point.

That Sunday we were at TMF. It wasn't a congregation of strangers to us. There were several cousins and friends from twenty years ago there—people we hadn't been in touch with since we left the farm. It felt good. After the service we met downstairs for coffee and cookies. This group liked to visit after the service. It was their summer schedule ... the first week of holidays! While all this was happening, I was approached and asked to join a group of three for a brief conversation. This was their search committee. I was very uncomfortable meeting in such a public space, but they assured me that no one would suspect anything was being set in motion. I was simply a visiting pastor, and the committee was seeking some advice. No one there suspected that this was the first contact with a prospective pastor. I briefly stated my dilemma of the timing of my term at Springstein. They understood, but we agreed to get back in touch later that fall. I was already wondering what I should do about this opportunity.

Judy and Ernie facing major project, June 1994

To figure out how to proceed, one of the first contacts I made was with John Wiebe, who was the Manitoba Conference pastor. His work was with congregations and pastors, assisting in the process of filling vacant pastoral positions and giving guidance so that everything was done properly. I shared with him the opportunity that had opened up and the dilemma with my term at Springstein. He said, "You've just agreed to a three-year term there! You have a commitment to fill. You can't leave. It's unethical." Or words to that effect. I told him I had made a commitment to start the term but had indicated that I might not complete it because I was feeling restless. He considered this information for a few minutes and then said that I had an "out." He didn't give me his blessing and wasn't happy with the case but would support me in the process.

Summer was over and the church schedule was taking on the regular fall to winter agenda. It was busy. The people from Mather contacted me to meet at Carman over coffee for further discussion. I went but was nervous about meeting in such a public place. What if some Springstein people happened by our table, wondering what was going on? That didn't happen, but I would continue to be nervous until I could declare our intentions to the congregation at Springstein.

Our discussion with the Mather group included my desire to take a part-time position. Would two thirds of a workload and salary be acceptable? Our plans were to possibly establish a sheep flock and do some farming. There was also a house to build. In that case, I would be a non-resident pastor, driving the twenty-five kilometres to Mather from our farm. In the past, pastors had always lived in or close to the church. But neither of these issues were seen as a problem. Harvest was beginning at Mather, so this would have to do for now. We needed to inform the Springstein congregation as soon as possible. I didn't want them to hear it from any other source.

I met with Ron Loeppky, the congregational chair. It was a surprise to him, but he quickly grasped the issues. After a while I asked him for his advice as to my path forward. I clearly remember these words: "Follow your heart." By this time, my ... our ... hearts were back at the farm. He, in effect, gave his blessing.

On the following Sunday after the benediction, I asked the people to stay for an announcement. It was very difficult for me to inform them of our plans. We had always been graciously treated; however, they came to accept our parting. We would be there for another eight months, till the end of June.

The months just before moving were busy and went by quickly. Judy and I planned how the move and getting settled would proceed. We had the house to dismantle and somehow had to build the new dwelling. Before this I had built barns and other outbuildings, but a house was another matter. We would need someone to draw up plans using the lumber we had saved. Judy was working at the CMBC bookstore at the time, and over coffee had chatted about our plans. Henry Loewen was a regular at coffee, and when he heard about plans of dismantling an old house, he became very interested. "You don't take down an old house; you restore it!" He had previous experience in re-construction. Judy came home week after week with the advice Henry was giving her. I finally said that if Henry wanted to save that house, he needed to come out to see it and give us advice as to whether it was feasible. He took us up on that challenge.

We went out to the farm, again on the May long weekend, and he met us there. The insides of the house had been removed, so a good assessment was possible. He took his time and then declared that it could be done. The house was basically square and quite sound. I said we'd need to move it onto a new foundation. At first he said there were people who could work with the old thick stone foundation and repair it. I claimed it would be difficult to insulate properly, so it needed to be moved. He finally agreed with my point. Years later when he and Cora spent a night in our B&B, we rehashed stories from the past. He admitted that he had approved the project while coming down the lane toward the yard. However, he had spent some time appraising the structure before pronouncing it feasible. He thought he would lack credibility if he spoke his judgement while stepping out of the car upon his arrival!

House being rejuvenated, October 1994

The decision was made! A major change in direction! It was now a renovation or restoration project. Later I thought that rejuvenation might capture it well. The path ahead was coming together. We'd settle in at Crystal City. A position at TMF had been secured. Dreams of establishing a flock of sheep and a B&B for Judy were on the horizon. Not sure exactly where or when the B&B idea was born, but it seemed a natural for Judy, so the big old house would be redesigned with this in mind. A major decision. Would it be a good one? In 2020 I would declare to Judy, "The two best decisions we've made were to leave the farm and to come back to the farm!" It takes a time of reflection and a certain stage of life to make such a declaration.

How did I come to this conclusion? Why was leaving the farm one of the two best decisions?

I'll provide a short response. Those twenty plus years after we left the farm encompassed such a vast richness of experience for us and our family. We met so many great people from a wide range of society. Yes, many were within the Mennonite milieu, but many were from outside that narrow range we had grown up with. Many of these people are still our close friends. Others we may not meet for years, then when we do, we immediately click! We had exposure to many people's lives—their triumphs and their defeats. Serving as a pastor provides a certain "in" to people's lives that would otherwise not be available. It would be difficult to imagine our lives without these experiences. I was also forced to learn to read material that I would never had read had I remained a farmer. This reading and commitment to life-long learning is something I wouldn't have wanted to miss.

So … one of our best decisions! The second-best decision was to come back. I trust that the stories told here of life on the farm in 1994 and following into retirement explain that decision as another best decision. We have been back for twenty-six years and have never second guessed or regretted this choice!

Coming Full Circle, Home

Where is one's home? I'd like to think we tried to be at home every place we lived, and I believe we achieved this. When we lived on our acreage at Swift Current, we would travel "home" to Manitoba to visit parents and relatives. Then, after the eight-hour trip back to our acreage, we were glad to be home again! However, there's something special about the place where one spent the first years of one's life. I had spent the first thirty years of my life in my "home" community. Judy spent her first six years at Morden, and then her family moved to Crystal City. This was her home for the next twenty-two years. When we left Springstein in 1994, we were moving home.

Much had changed in the twenty-two years we'd been away, just as we had changed. When we left, we had three pre-school age children. We came back, still being parents, but ones with an "empty nest." In fact, we had no children living in Manitoba. Michelle and Don were in the Maldive Islands for the next year, and Jason had just left for Ontario, where he would study Computer Science at the University of Waterloo. Rhonda and John had settled in Saskatchewan, and Duane was establishing his business in Calgary. However, we were near our parents, who had retired from their farms and were living in town. All four were still relatively healthy and were excited to have us back home. We had realized when we had contemplated the move back that we would be closer to our aging parents and would be an additional support to that which our siblings were already providing.

We had our major construction projects in mind as we moved back, but first we had to set up camp. The garage we hoped to live in that winter was just a plan on a piece of paper. I had bought a large used canvas tent, which would be an upgrade from the pup tent we had used the previous two summers.

Our parents: Margaret Hildebrand, Beth and Dick Zacharias, and Jacob Hildebrand

We moved our queen-size bed into this tent. I said if we were going to be working hard the next months, an air mattress was not sufficient to get a good night's sleep. The bed took up most of the room, but we were basically living outside anyway. There was room for a small bookshelf. I needed a place for books and papers, for I would be starting my pastoral duties before we'd move out of this tent. We managed to get hydro to install temporary outlets for power, and Manitoba Telephone strung an above-ground wire in the ditch from the neighbours over a mile away. We needed a phone desperately, for we would be coordinating all kinds of activities over the next months. We also had a picnic shelter in case of rain and a fridge for our food! We built an outdoor shower! We filled a black plastic container, holding three to four gallons of water, from the creek in the morning and placed it in direct sunlight for the day. It had a spout with a shower head. By evening, the water was nice and warm, and we enjoyed our "solar shower!"

If we monitored it carefully, there was just enough for both of us. Our gas camp stove and our barbecue determined our diet. We were set up under the trees and surrounded by nature.

One morning, we heard a "meowing." We thought it was a kitten, but when we listened more closely, we saw the tiny fawn in the grass very close to our campsite. Then we noticed its mother a little further away, beckoning the fawn to follow her. What a great way to start a morning! This would be our residence until late fall when our garage would be ready to move into for the winter. There was a cold spell toward the end. We would have our breakfast dressed in heavy coveralls! It was an enjoyable experience, for the most part. The hailstorm mid-August interfered for a brief spell, since our tent had a rip in it that needed repair. We lost all our leaf cover on the trees, and all the birds disappeared. We spent two nights with Judy's folks until we could get camp restored. The setting was no longer the same, but we adjusted, even having friends from Springstein joining us for a weekend. While we had no regrets concerning the tenting, we rarely tented after that when we went on holidays.

We would move into our restored house on July 31, 1995 (our anniversary). I suggested that we should set up our tent for old times' sake on our next anniversary, but then it seemed to be too much effort!

We had to focus on two distinct aspects of our new venture. There was our farmyard with the building plans, the establishing of a sheep enterprise, and the B&B. Then there was the aspect of becoming the pastor of Trinity Mennonite Fellowship. I was due to start responsibilities by mid-August. This gave us six weeks to get established on the farm. It was a two-thirds time position, and we needed to determine what that meant. A pastor friend of mine in the Elm Creek area was farming and serving as pastor in this kind of arrangement. He told me that one could calculate how many blocks of time constituted full-time work and then work out the pattern for two-thirds time. A block would be a morning, afternoon, or evening time period. I proposed this method to the leadership at Trinity. I also proposed that I would work closer to full time in the winter months and something like half-time in the five months of summer and fall. This all met with their immediate approval. Trinity was a farming community, so the church programming was fairly relaxed in the summer due to the busy farming schedule. I kept track of the blocks I spent working for the church and would report this to the council periodically, but no one ever questioned my schedule. My work ethic made sure that I would not shortchange the congregation. I had, I considered, worked too hard at Springstein. Now I could give total effort of two-thirds time to the church and have one-third to provide balance to my life! It became a very good arrangement for me. There was enough mental stimulation and lots of time for physical work. Mind and body together were good for the soul! Both I considered to be exercises of spirituality!

Trinity was a newer congregation with only an eighteen-year history when we moved there. There had been four pastors serving the congregation previous to my coming. Trinity was almost the direct opposite of Springstein. There was little specific tradition that needed to be followed. Instead of instructing me on how things had always been done, they were quite prepared to have me do it "my way" and then make adjustments if necessary. They were totally open to innovation and experimentation.

Trinity had been formed due to a split within the Mather Mennonite Church. These people experienced what too many Mennonite congregations did. A long-term pastor at Springstein, Elder W. Enns, had resigned his position after thirty-five years of service because of a church conflict. He laments, "What causes Mennonites to quarrel so bitterly and usually end the quarrel by splitting into two groups? Why do we, with our peace emphasis, find it so hard to reconcile and reach out in understanding and forgiving love once again?" These questions continue to plague Mennonite people. It's been called a "Mennonite disease." I won't attempt to answer those questions. I don't think that conflict is necessarily reserved for our churches alone. At a ministerial meeting with fellow pastors from United and Anglican congregations, I suggested that Mennonites were dedicated "church goers!" So when there is conflict, one group leaves to start a new congregation. They can't not go to church! I had observed that in their traditions, when a family experiences conflict, they simply quit going to church, period. The pastors thought I had nailed it! The members who formed Trinity longed for a more intimate expression of faith. There had been a great deal of societal change in the 1960s and 70s, which affected the churches as well. The rigid nature of some congregations couldn't cope with this change, so splits, in some cases, were almost inevitable. Conflict is by no means restricted to church life. There's lots of evidence of conflicts between neighbouring communities that has nothing to do with religion!

Trinity people worked hard at becoming a fellowship. The wish was that all would be involved and all voices would be heard. Issues were to be decided by trying to reach a consensus rather than a strict majority vote. Different understandings of faith, belief, and lifestyle were considered, and people weren't easily threatened by differences of opinion. Conflicts, when they arose, were dealt with. We didn't come to Trinity as strangers. I knew a lot of the people from our earlier life in the area. Many I hadn't had contact with for over twenty years, so we had some catching up to do. I had several relatives there: an aunt and uncle, and cousins both from the Hildebrand and Harms sides of my family. Judy had a brother and his family, as well as some second cousins. Being related to so many might have become an issue, but it never did.

One of my first official functions was to officiate at a child dedication service for two infants who had been born that spring. The parents had waited for my arrival. I was related to both! On another occasion, a young couple came back to our church to have their daughter dedicated. I had officiated at their wedding. The mother had grown up in this church, and her parents and brothers were still in the community. They didn't have a close connection to a church where they were living. I consented to do this and had planned the regular way I was used to conducting this service. A few days before the service was to take place, I was informed that the husband's parents and an assortment of other relatives, including grandparents, would be in attendance. They were an Anglican family who practised infant baptism in their tradition. I thought I better upgrade what I had intended to do. I added more "pomp and ceremony!" The service was well received.

Another young woman came back to the Mather community to celebrate her wedding. She had attended Sunday school in Trinity, but otherwise her family had little connection to our church. To have a church wedding was important to her. She was an only child of a rather wealthy farmer (a cousin of mine). He would go all out, with little expense spared for the wedding. He had rented a limo from Winnipeg to transport the bridal party from the farm south of Mather to Crystal City Mennonite Church, where the ceremony was to take place. We were all in place at the church, but where was the bride? A wedding guest, who was himself late in arriving at the church, informed me that he had seen a limo heading west a few minutes ago. We waited some forty minutes. The groom was sweating, and I was trying to keep everyone calm. I spoke with the limo driver after the ceremony, and he explained that there were no street signs out in the country. How was he to know where to go? I suggested a professional driver would make sure of the route ahead of time!

Another bride at a wedding in Winnipeg (while I was at Springstein) was so nervous, the bridesmaids couldn't get her out of the washroom in the basement of the church. That ceremony started twenty minutes late, and the pianist kept playing music while the people waited. Two days later, I was in Winnipeg to get a licence renewed. The person at the desk was that same pianist! I commended her on her ability to carry on through the delay. She said something about having seen it all! Winnipeg wasn't as big as I had been led to believe. Imagine meeting this pianist in such a different setting. She hadn't recognized me!

While I was largely responsible for the Sunday worship services at Trinity, others were in charge of special services. The annual church picnic was one of these. The picnic was centred on the Sunday school kids, so their teachers along with the Education Committee members did the planning. I became aware that the plan was for the children to do a short play with the setting being at a creek bank. The teachers were wondering how to create the scene if the event was to take place in the church. I suggested that the picnic could take place at our farm. I had a specific place in mind that would work quite well. It was our first spring/summer back at the farm, and our renovation projects were still ongoing. This would also give an opportunity for the congregation to get a sense of what we were doing. The day arrived. It was a little chilly, but the senior members came dressed for the weather. They set up their lawn chairs at the top of the bank. Others came and found a place to sit, some on blankets on the slope. The play took place at the edge of the creek. It was a narrow stream at this place, and the kids could easily cross it if they so desired. As the play progressed, some younger boys, not yet in Sunday school and thus not part of the cast, wandered down to the creek. With sticks in their hands, they poked around in the water and explored, as boys tend to do. Their improvisation added an unexpected dimension to the whole morning! This kind of experience is difficult to duplicate. It was a special event for all.

One of the seniors would later tell me that he and other seniors wondered what the two of us were thinking in restoring such a large house. When he found out that a B&B was in the plans, he was relieved and told me, "Now it makes some sense! We were wondering about you!"

Winters offered another option to host the congregation. This time, plans were underway for the annual Christmas Eve service. The plan was to enact some scenes ahead of time for a nativity slide show. Kids would be dressed as shepherds, angels, magi, and Joseph and Mary. Photos would be taken and fashioned into a slide set. This would then be presented in the church on Christmas Eve. Our yard and sheep barn were chosen as the site to take these pictures. Some of the poor, lightly dressed angels, almost froze as their scenes were captured on film. It was a cold day, and there was a considerable amount of snow on the ground. The barn was a bit warmer. Sheep were penned up next to the manger scene. They were tame enough so that the kids could pet them and feed them some alfalfa!

The production was a great success! Our yard would be used for several more such events. The sheep and the creek were attractions, and the yard lent itself well to the various age groups. The older folk could visit in the shade of the old maple trees, and the younger ones could go for walks in the pasture. One summer, a family who had moved to a new location in a very scenic area on the shore of a lake offered to host the annual picnic. It was a considerable distance to drive, but people came in full numbers. This family had purchased a few sheep from me, and I would shear them each summer. Since they were now farther away, I offered to bring my shearing equipment and shearing clothes along and shear the sheep after the picnic! Some others stayed to watch. I served as shepherd for both my flocks that Sunday!

The movement of people out of rural areas resulted in a declining population, which impacting Trinity. Three couples retired from farming and moved to Brandon and Winnipeg just before our arrival. They didn't have children in the area to carry on the farm. Young people tended not to stay in the area after completing high school. Many went to university or found employment in the cities. Families were smaller, and farms were becoming larger. Some people stopped attending church. More of the members became grandparents and would tend to be away more often visiting their grandchildren in the city. Some became "snowbirds," spending the winters down south. Our seniors were getting older. Not many funerals had been held the first two decades of Trinity's existence, but now they were becoming frequent in our midst. Yet the congregation was facing the future and making adjustments to accommodate the declining membership. Financial support remained strong. We became used to a smaller group attending the worship services. Fortunately, we had very good singers so that even with fewer people, we still filled the space with sound!

Ernie and Judy, 2000

I was approaching sixty years of age. I wanted to retire at this age and then farm on a small scale in a more relaxed way. I had given my notice to resign, and it was accepted. Eight years was longer than previous pastors had served. I didn't get the sense that people were tired of me. It was more that I got tired of myself in the role in their midst. It was my longest stay in any congregation. I had a number of weddings to officiate that summer. It seemed that couples thought they better get married before I retired. My final service was to be the end of August. The thought crossed my mind that the congregation would likely have a farewell gathering for us. I thought it would likely take the form of a low-key potluck meal and then maybe a speech or two. I really hadn't given it much thought and wasn't expecting to be on the planning committee!

It was August. People were coming off holidays and preparing for the upcoming harvest. Most of our children and grandchildren were with us for a weekend in mid-August. On Sunday morning, some of our kids were preparing to get a start for home, and others would accompany us to church. I didn't have any responsibility in the service that morning. I had conducted the last wedding the day before. We left for church, and just before we reached the #3 junction to head west toward Mather, a familiar looking red car turned the corner just ahead of us. It was some distance ahead, but I said it was Jason and Katharina's car! They lived in Winnipeg and hadn't been out for the weekend. What were they up to? We never caught up to the red Colt, but we did see it turn off the highway into Mather. So it was our kids from Winnipeg? What was going on? As we approached the church, we saw the church yard full of cars! Normally there would have been approximately a dozen vehicles. I spotted my brother-in-law's Ford truck with "Bill Klassen Auctions" painted on the side. It dawned on us! It's a surprise retirement event! We had never suspected! The church was packed as we were ushered to a seat reserved for us. There were people there from Springstein, and all our children were there. The ones who had told us they needed to head for home had misled us! It was all too much for me to comprehend. I don't take surprises all that well, I realized, and that was confirmed with a surprise seventieth birthday party ten years later. But it was a great service with the theme, "The Winds of Change." After the service there was a noon meal for all the guests in the hall, followed by a pastor and spouse "roast" of sorts. All very supportive. Osler Mennonite had sent a one-page greeting. Michelle and Jason reflected on our journey as a family. While Judy and I were completely surprised by this celebration, I believe the congregation was even more surprised that they were able to do all this planning without us hearing a whisper!

My eight years as pastor at Trinity ended. Upon consulting the daily planners that I had used all those years, the following was revealed: a list of the variety of activities that I needed to keep track of. There were just slight changes over the eight years, so these activities were noted: worship planning meeting, hospital visit, release rams, council meeting, curling bonspiel, funeral planning, Mom's birthday, auction sale, Grey Cup Day, faspa at the Thiessens', Rock Lake Hospital meeting, wedding, Molly (our dog) to the vet, leave for the west (visit children), pastors' meeting, wool loading day, Valdy concert, afternoon study, Cartwright Seniors sleigh ride, Sheep Days in Brandon, etc. That was my life. There was a rich balance of farming, church, and community involvements. I never made any entries in the mood indicator log that I had kept before. I had achieved the balance I needed for healthy living!

David and Romaine's wedding, Ernie officiating, 2002

We had indeed established our life on our farm parallel with our involvement with Trinity. Our restoration project was more or less completed the first year of our coming home. Yard landscaping needed to follow. I would use almost all of the implements that had come with the purchase of the tractor. I used the tiller, the scraper, the set of harrows and the front-end loader to prepare the lawn for seeding. By the following spring (1996), we had our first crop of lambs, and our B&B had welcomed our first guests! We needed the use of some of the crop land that Harv had been cropping, so our land base became the home quarter section of land. We needed these fields to grow alfalfa for the sheep's winter feed. The pasture had until now been rented to a neighbour for his cattle. I now used it for our sheep. The fences all needed to be upgraded for the sheep. The page wire fences we had left in 1971 were still in evidence but in poor repair. I found that the Polypay sheep were much easier on fences than the Suffolk sheep had been. This new flock always moved as a flock, while the Suffolk would be scattered all over the pasture and always looking for an escape route! The Polypay did get out on occasion, and then they were all out at the same time! Livestock in fences continually present challenges!

A farm needed a dog, and we got Molly without really looking for her. We attended the fair at Crystal City the second summer that we were back. There was a litter of pups at the petting zoo, and they were for sale at $5.00 each. We went home with a friendly, black pup who would love to dig in our new yard! We were told she was an English Sheep Dog/German Shepherd cross. She loved the farm and found her place. She wasn't a herding dog or a sheep guard dog. She was just a dog-dog. She loved to go with me to the hay field. The first month we had her, she followed me around a twelve-acre field as I mowed the second cut of alfalfa. It was a dangerous venture for a young pup to be following a sickle mower, but we managed without mishap. Over the next years, she always insisted on accompanying me in all the haying operations, often catching a ride with me in the cab of the truck. When I upgraded the truck to a somewhat newer model, I insisted that she ride in the back. She tended to shed a lot of hair. She wasn't impressed with the change, but we went out to the field. I started on my first round in the field, and she remained on the back of the truck. As I finished the round, I noted with surprise that she was sitting in the cab with a big smile on her face! The back window of the cab featured sliding windows, and although they had been closed, the window was not latched. Molly, with either her nose or her paw, had managed to slide the window open and crawl into the cab. She was proud of her accomplishment, and after that, she rode in the cab and I used the vacuum more frequently!

One year in early spring, when there was still some snow on the ground, Judy and I went for a walk in the pasture near to the place where we would later establish a new yard. Of course, Molly was with us. We were up on a bank overlooking the creek and the neighbour's pasture beyond when we noted a rabbit hurriedly bouncing along, with Molly in hot pursuit. I said to Judy, "Poor Molly. She'll chase rabbits all her life and never catch one!" Molly was losing distance as the rabbit approached a barb wire fence and slowed down a bit so as to jump through without hitting a wire. The rabbit misjudged its leap and hit a wire. As it was thrown back, Molly grabbed it with her teeth and wouldn't let go. The rabbit was a goner! After a brief struggle, Molly carried the rabbit back toward our yard in her teeth with her head held high. Her tail was also held aloft, a stance I had never seen before. What a dog!

We added a team of horses to our farm. I had become aware of a breed called Norwegian Fjords. They were mid-size horses with a gentle disposition but known for their pulling power. I remembered growing up with harness horses and thought a team would fit into our farm rather well. The option of buggy rides in the summer and sleigh rides in the winter was appealing. It would be an added attraction for B&B guests and thus even revenue bearing. Rhonda scouted out this option and informed me that there was a breeder at Killarney who had this breed. We knew where his ranch was, so on our way back from Brandon, having delivered a load of lambs, we stopped by to inquire about this breed and our interest in a team. The owner looked a little puzzled. He had just placed an ad in the farm paper listing a young team for sale but knew the paper had not yet been delivered! How did I know about this team? It just happened that way! The price was in our range, so this became a viable option. His wife had insisted that their policy was to do a site visit before every sale. Almost like infant adoption procedures! After some more conversation, that requirement was deleted. He discovered that I was related to the owner of the John Deere dealership just down the road from his ranch. He knew this owner, my cousin, was trustworthy, and he determined that I was of the same stock! The purchase was completed. We had left home with a trailer load of lambs to sell and came home having purchased a team of horses! The income from the lambs didn't match the expense of the horses, but that's farming!

The rancher and his wife delivered the team later that week. His wife declared that the horses would love it here when she saw the yard and the pasture down to the creek. This would be their home. They were a young team, and thus we would need to wait some time before they could be trained to harness. We could lead them and get to know them, but training would have to wait till the fall or winter. I went back to the rancher to purchase a set of harnesses and other related gear. I purchased a sleigh at an auction sale, and my brother-in-law gave me an old stone boat that would be good to start with. I knew nothing about training horses, but I would harness them and hook them up to the sled once we had snow. They were exceptionally calm and gentle, just as advertised. But I couldn't get them to move once they were hitched up. They just stood there! So different from the teams I had encountered years ago. I soon concluded that training was beyond my capability.

A friend informed me of a person who trained horses not that far away. I contacted him in early December, and he was willing to train my team. He had a five-week program that he followed to accomplish a thorough training. I told him that four weeks of training would allow us to get the horses back to our yard for Christmas. I was anxious to offer sleigh rides for the family during that season. I explained that the team was gentle and already used to being harnessed, but he wasn't convinced. He said he needed five weeks. He had a trailer, so he offered to pick them up and told me to come after a few weeks to note the progress. I did that on a very cold December day. His yard was well sheltered. We harnessed up the team and then put them through their paces. It was remarkable. He would have them walk and then gave the command to trot and they followed all his instructions. At the end of the session, he told me that he'd return them after four weeks of training! He was impressed with the breed.

At Christmas, I hitched them up to the stone boat and gave rides in circles around the barnyard. There was quite a bit of snow, so I and the passengers got a fair dose of it! Susanna was not yet a year old when she got her first ride. The next summer, I had acquired a buckboard at another auction sale, so rides were provided along the country roads. A buckboard is a cross between a buggy and a wagon. It was equipped with springs, so there was some bounce to the ride. Susanna did not yet have expansive language skills but could communicate quite effectively. She'd come to me and say, "Papa" and then snort like a horse and bounce up and down. Her signal that she wanted a ride. What grandpa could refuse such a request?

Favourite summer activity, 2002

Our family dynamic changed during these first eight years back on the farm. Duane and Andrea's wedding took place at Calgary in August 1995. That was the same weekend we picked up the rams at Magrath on our way home! Jason had found his life partner, Katharina, in Germany, and they were now living in Winnipeg. Susanna, our first granddaughter, was born early in 2000 to Don and Michelle. When all of these people, together with John and Rhonda and Noah and Jem from Saskatchewan, came home, our large farmhouse was nearly full! The grandchildren added a lot of new life to a family that had been mainly adults for many years. Noah and Jem could get into a lot of mischief. Judy caught them just in time one day, disrupting their plan to place Susanna, a one-year-old, in a wagon and push her down the hill just west of the house!

Judy faced the challenge of making sure she knew when the family was coming home so that she wouldn't take reservations for B&B guests at the same time. Family took priority! One summer, we had a large gathering of our family as well as Judy's family on our yard. There were tents set up all over the yard for the three-day event. On Sunday afternoon, she received a phone call requesting a room for the night. A young couple from England had been touring rural Manitoba in hopes of finding a farm and moving to Canada. They were desperate for a room. It was a long weekend, and no hotel rooms were available. We still had one room in the house not occupied, so Judy told them they could come. They joined our extended family around a campfire that evening and fit right in! They were full of stories of their travels and experiences!

Flexibility allowed this great experience. In some ways, I suppose, that was our code of operation all along. Early retirement would likely be more of the same!

Life as a Student

Elfrieda and I were walking up the hill west of the barnyard. It was fall, and we had been playing down by the creek She was five years old, and I was three. She told me, "Tomorrow I'm going to school and will be away all day." I couldn't believe it. My playmate would be gone, and I'd be on my own. Life would never be the same.

Two years later, it was my turn to head to school. I was six years old and would be seven before Christmas. Boys born late in the fall were thought too immature to start school at five years of age. We'd see. I was going up the steps of the elementary school when I met some of my cousins. I was excited to see them and greeted them in German. One of them warned me not to speak German in school. Here the English language was to be used. I had learned some English from a hired man staying with us the previous winter. I think his name was Tony Penner. I had a limited English vocabulary that I could use but was likely too shy to speak much anyway.

There were two large classrooms in that school. Up the stairs, in through the big doors and to the right was the Grade One and Two classroom. Miss Gillbert was the teacher. She'd been there for many years and would stay for several more. She had never married and had white hair. She was strict. There was a strap hanging in the corner of the room, and she would use it. It struck fear in my heart. Some of the boys got strapped. I don't recall the reason other than they misbehaved. It seemed the same ones every time.

Some would smirk coming back to their desks. They were used to it. No big deal. Wouldn't admit that it hurt. I never got the strap.

I was learning to read. Dick and Jane stories with their dog, Spot. Reading wasn't too hard to learn. We were taught to sound out the words. If we couldn't figure out the word, we only had to ask once. Memories were good at that age. We were told by other students that we would have to learn to spell and also do arithmetic. That would be very hard, we were told. One could never ease up, it seemed. There was always something more to learn. We were told that certain grades ahead were very hard. I think Grade Five was on of those. Later in high school, Grade Ten or Eleven were deemed to be tough years.

I settled in and must have been a good student who found learning not to be that difficult. Some students were known to have skipped a whole grade due to their high marks. I wasn't offered to skip a grade, but three of us were offered a faster track so that we'd complete three grades in two years. It must have been Grade Six when we re-joined a regular class. This is confirmed by an old report card from the school year 1952–53. Miss Garrett, the teacher wrote, "If Ernie continues to work hard, he'll clear Grade Five by June. He is a good worker." In June, the report certifies this promotion to Grade Six (with honours). Checking this report card revealed several surprises to me. I had high marks in spelling and writing. The experience of writing this account informs me that I would be in serious trouble without the capable editing of Judy, whose strength is in these subjects. Also spell check! My weakest subject was arithmetic. I would have thought these would have been just the opposite. There is also a Character Record on the card. The headings include the following: Health, Thrift, Reliability, Social Attitude, Clear Thinking. I was graded with an "A" in all these categories in each of the three reporting periods. I'm relieved not to have report cards from my time in high school! I'm sure some of those wouldn't be so positive. Anyway, I went from being one of the oldest in my grade to being one of the youngest. This would be the case throughout public school and even university.

My student life in Grade Six was very different from what I might have expected. At the end of August, I suffered my near fatal farm accident and spend two weeks in the hospital and then considerable time recovering at home. This was followed by surgery in November. (I recall the month because the Grey Cup was being played. Winnipeg lost, and Mom told me of a scene she had seen on Portage Avenue. A distraught fan mourned the loss by crawling on his knees for several blocks on the sidewalk! Or something like that. I wasn't a football fan at that age. I checked my memory with the book *100 Grey Cups* by Stephen Brunt. Sure enough, in the 1953 Grey Cup, the score was Hamilton 12 and Winnipeg 6. I would be turning eleven years old in a few days.) A second surgery followed in a few months, which meant missing more school. My marks suffered, but I don't have report cards from that year. I did make up marks the following months. At the end of June, I was awarded a watch for being the "Most Improved Student!" I thought the award was suspect. It was only due to my three hospital stays, missing a lot of school and thus getting low grades, that I was able to improve during the last four months of the year!

That first year after the accident was difficult for me. I had to adjust to having missed so much school and also to my self image. My face was disfigured. I still have the school photo taken that year some time before Christmas. I compare it to the one from the year before the accident. I don't recall more than one reaction from classmates, but the one was painful, even though I shrugged it off. An older student, a known bully, said to me, "I hate you. You're ugly. I wish you would have died!" Thankfully, this was the only such experience. I had enough dealing with my own self view and didn't need reminders from others.

Bullying was just the nature of school life. It wasn't called that then. I didn't experience much of it, other than the occasional time on the school bus. There were a few Mennonite kids on the bus, and most were the "English." We got along fine most of the time, but quite quickly conflict could happen, and if it was with a Mennonite kid, accusations of being Nazis would fly. It had just been a few years since the end of World War Two. Mennonites were pacifists and had conscientious objector status with the government. Other kids' families had suffered loss of relatives, uncles, grandfathers in the wars. We were German and thought to be sympathetic to the enemy. I believe it was a few of these incidents that caused me to vow to give up the German language.

Bullying went both ways. One is bullied, and one bullies others. There was a family in town considered to be the poorest of the poor. I'm unsure of all the details, but their shack had been moved out of town to the edge of the town dump. One of the girls from this family was in my classroom and was continually teased: "She has fleas, she has fleas!" And we would run away from her. Most of the class engaged in this behaviour. I did too, though inwardly I had sympathy for her. Little good that did her. Another time I was caught with a few other boys picking on younger kids in the school yard and harassing them. This went on for some time until we were caught. My parents were called in to meet with me and the principal. A severe warning was issued. The gossip on the school grounds was that we could be sent to reform school. It didn't come close to that, but the scare I received taught me a lesson. I wasn't nearly the good kid that my Grade Five card reported. I wonder today when people talk about their experiences of being bullied. Those having been bullied speak of their experience, but the ones that bully never do. It's difficult to recount this part of one's school life.

My scholastic achievement likely peaked in Grade Five. My attitude changed as the years went by. I did enough to get reasonable marks but had no ambition for high ones. My "clear thinking" was serving me well. I reasoned that I was within the top quarter of the class. If they fail me, all those below me would fail as well, and I couldn't see that happening. School and studying became a burden. I much more preferred to be at home working on the farm. I would miss a few weeks of school to help with the harvest in fall and the seeding in spring. Dad approved of this, but Mom had her doubts. This pattern caught up with me in Grades Ten and Eleven. I never tried to catch up with the material that I had missed. In some subjects like history it didn't matter so much; however, in chemistry, geometry, and algebra it mattered a great deal. In physics I missed the section on electricity, and to this day don't understand it. But on the exam, I knew the rest of the material, so my mark was the highest of any subject. In Grade Eleven, most of my marks were in the 50s. I had a 78 in physics, and I failed French—the only failed grade in ten years of schooling. Remember, I'd completed three grades in two years previously.

What to do after Grade Eleven? I was sixteen years old, and I was determined not to go back for Grade Twelve. I knew that I wouldn't be able to succeed because of the subjects I was struggling in. A friend of mine had access to a U of M catalogue and was checking out the Degree in Agriculture program. He mentioned to me that there was a two-year offering geared toward people anticipating farming as a career, as well as options in agri-business. I was intrigued. One didn't need Grade Twelve but would have to apply and be interviewed by a committee who would decide on one's eligibility.

I applied and later sat before this group of older, cigar-smoking university professors. I was only sixteen. I remember only one distinct question that was asked that puzzled me. It was about egg marketing boards. I didn't have a clue but made some response, possibly related to hog marketing. Anyway, I was accepted and was due in Winnipeg the first week of October 1959. I got a ride to the city with my Uncle Albert, who lived there. As we entered the city, he told me where I could catch a bus to take me to the university the next morning. He had to leave for work much earlier, so he couldn't take me. He parked his car in the back lane of his dwelling. It seems to me it might have been in the Wolseley area. I needed to transfer buses at Pembina Highway.

The next morning after having my own breakfast, I left the house. I had no idea where I was, but I must have wandered around until I noted a familiar street. I had to ask the bus driver which way to the university. He told me to hop in and then explained the transfers I would need to take. Upon arrival on the campus, I faced a similar experience. I had no idea where the agriculture buildings were. A big old building had the inscription, "School of Agriculture" way up on top. I thought this must be it, so I entered; however, it was now an administration building and likely had been one of the original buildings on campus. I was offered a map of the campus and pointed in a direction. By evening I had registered, met some fellow students, and secured my room in the men's residence. A whole group of us were placed in one hallway on the lower (basement) level of the residence. My roommate was Jim Pyott, a twenty-eight-year-old student from Roblin, Manitoba. We developed a good friendship, and he's the only student I stayed in touch with over the next sixty years. We noted that when someone had a birthday, they would be tossed in a bathtub full of cold water, fully clothed. It was hard to avoid such a fate. Jim and I vowed not to tell anyone our birth date but agreed to share our dates and keep that from others. What a joke! We were both born on December 5! That served us well, and years later led to an annual phone call on our birthdays!

Back to that first week. My uncle brought me my suitcase the first evening. I shared with him how my journey to the campus had gone! I think he was relieved that I'd found my way. He'd had a similar journey years before when he'd left Snowflake to study engineering at this same place. He left behind six brothers, who all remained in the farming business. He'd been very much on his own to find his way. We made arrangements to travel back home that weekend, since it was Thanksgiving. I believe the rest of the week was mainly orientation with regular classes to begin the next week. I realized that a four-hour block of classes was scheduled for Saturday mornings, so trips back home wouldn't happen often. I'm not sure if I went home again before Christmas, so the ride home the coming weekend would be good.

We departed Friday after my uncle's workday was over. It was raining and cold, but the trip proceeded well until we topped the valley after La Riviere and were met with a blast of snow that got heavier all the way to Crystal City. The streets in town were barely passable. We stopped at my grandparents' place. Uncle Albert had already decided to immediately head back to the city. I might have called home from there to let my parents know of our change of plans. So we headed back. It was slow going, and we got stuck in the snow just before the valley. There were other stuck cars there, and we helped each other out. None of us were dressed for the weather. After the valley, the weather reverted to rain, and it was clear sailing! Parts of western Manitoba received over twenty inches of snow. It's still a record snowfall for October to this day, sixty years later. The harvest hadn't been completed, and Dad still had flax to combine. He managed to hire a self-propelled combine to harvest the standing flax later that month. The temperatures were -20 F. Not pleasant at all. I don't recall how I spent that long weekend in the city. I suppose many of the other diploma students were there as well. Many were from western parts of the province, where the bulk of the snow had fallen.

The diploma course had been revised the previous year to reflect the changes in agriculture. According to the transcript I still have, there were a total of twenty-eight courses over four semesters. Several subjects ran for two semesters. There were no electives. All the twenty-two enrolled students took every subject. All the students were male, although there were a few female students in the degree program. To have any was a rarity. That has changed remarkably by now. The subjects ranged from Insects, to Soils, to Farm Law, to Farm Power Machinery, to Crops. There were also courses on Citizenship and Communication. It was in Communication that I discovered my ability and freedom to engage in public speaking. I seldom experienced undue nervousness. Of course, I didn't realize that this course would, in large part, lead me to a future vocation. Decades later, I would attribute the Communication and the Sheep Management courses to having had a lasting impact on me.

I was the youngest student enrolled. Several had a few years of farming experience. One was a married student with a family. I studied hard and my grades were much better than in high school. They ranged from 62 to 82 per cent. If I had been more mature, I would have learned much more. In later years I would remark that I was glad I started studies in agriculture at sixteen and studies in theology at twenty-eight years of age, instead of the other way round. I'm fearful of how little I would have learned in theology at sixteen!

I didn't engage in much of the social life on campus. I attended sporting events like hockey and basketball on campus. A number of my fellow students were Bombers fans, so we ventured way out to the old Blue Bombers stadium in the Polo Park area to cheer on the team. One November we attended a playoff game in frigid temperatures. We nearly froze, and the Bombers lost in a very low scoring game. Fewer than eight points were scored, combined.

A church service was offered in the residence every Sunday. Clergy from the city would come in the afternoon to conduct these services. Some Sundays I would venture to attend Bethel Mennonite Church just off Pembina Highway. The bus route provided good access, but the schedule was reduced on Sundays. I had to hurry after the service to catch the bus back to campus so as not to miss the noon meal. One Sunday I was late. I saw the bus depart before I could get there. I would have to wait forty-five minutes for the next one. It was much too far to walk, so I settled into my wait. Shortly after, a big black car pulled over to the curb, and the driver beckoned me over and asked if I needed a ride to the campus. When I nodded yes, he said, "Get in." He was also dressed for church, and he said he lived on campus. I thought he looked familiar, and he turned out to be Dr. Hugh Saunderson, president of the university! He told me he often stopped to pick up those who looked like students along that route home from his church! I didn't miss lunch after all.

I'll mention two highlights for me. One was the tour of rural Manitoba that we took in the summer of 1960. We were exposed to the varieties of farming enterprises that existed from the Red River Valley and out west as far as Melita. We went by bus, and the trip lasted ten days. We stayed in hotels and most meals were in restaurants. Others were hosted by the farming families we were visiting. We were required to keep notes and write a report. Other than that, it seemed like a holiday. The second highlight was the train trip to Fort William and Port Arthur (now Thunder Bay) that fall to explore grain marketing. We toured the grain terminals and also a large ocean-going ship that was being loaded with wheat for the export market. All expenses for these two ventures were included in our tuition fees at the beginning of the year.

Dad had offered to pay the tuition as well as room and board for the two years. Upon enrollment, we were offered bursaries from the Department of Agriculture. These bursaries would be forgiven if students returned to farming for the next three years. What a gift! I had full intention of returning to the farm, so the whole two-year experience ended up costing Dad very little.

In early April 1961, I received my Diploma in Agriculture. My parents came into Winnipeg for the ceremony and then to take me home. My dad was one who didn't mind chatting with strangers. He met Professor Leonard Siemens, who had been one of my profs. As a parting comment, he told Dad, within my hearing, that if I had learned how little I knew and how much there was still to learn, then they had reached their objective. I had also been told that good farming should provide a good living and improve the soil. A worthy objective. Now, back home to the farm and the rest of my life. My formal educational venture was over, or so I thought! It was time for seeding!

September 1971, ten years later, I was back in the classroom at CMBC studying theology. Elsewhere in this story, I have related how we came to this decision. This was a whole new experience. I was twenty-eight, married to Judy, with three children in tow. While many of the students were there straight out of high school, there were also a number of married students, and some with children. We felt a welcome on campus and quickly formed friendships. Since harvest and fall work hadn't been completed, we would travel back to the farm on weekends to complete these tasks well into October. That made for a very busy schedule, as I was enrolled with a full load and was just learning how to read "heavy stuff" and write term papers.

I had two concerns at the time. One was the suggestion made by certain leaders in our home congregation that the professors at this college were suspect in offering false doctrine. I listened carefully, not that sure what I should listen for. Would I be able to detect it if there was some? I soon relaxed. The teaching was solid, and the professors were kind, gentle people who were interested in getting to know us and guide us in learning and understanding the subjects they were teaching. I recall one incident in which a group of us "older' students were in the coffee room one evening. Several of us were wondering about the Old Testament course we were taking. It was so confusing. The OT prof happened to stop by, which was outside of character. He wasn't one to banter with a group of students. He asked us gathered there, "What are you understanding about what I'm teaching you?" We were stunned. We hadn't expected a snap test like this! A few of us uttered a few words. He replied, "Your getting it" and left the room. Wow, we knew something but didn't know we knew it. A relief of sorts, yet troubling. A lot of learning would be of that nature.

The second concern I had throughout the whole first year was my status as a mature student.

This status would need to be removed in order to continue the second year. We were allowed to attempt four courses and then select the three best ones to achieve a C average. These were courses cross registered with the U of M. I was assured it wouldn't be difficult, but I was only taking three courses that were eligible for this. I would need to pass all three. After the first semester and having received my grades from the exams, I thought I was on track, so I relaxed somewhat. It wasn't until June when I received my final marks in the mail that this concern was laid to rest. I had achieved a B+ in two courses and a B in the third. Now as a regular student, it would be clear sailing.

The next two years went by rather quickly. I really appreciated most of the classes and felt they were serving me well in the goal of entering church ministry. Courses in Bible, theology, and Anabaptist history were especially relevant, but I greatly valued Western history, sociology, philosophy, and logic as well. It wasn't a fully rounded education, but it also wasn't restricted to religious subjects. Integration of knowledge across disciplines was encouraged. We were learning to become critical thinkers, though we didn't realize it at the time. (Maybe this was what some back home had feared. We would learn to think! Ha, ha!)

To meet graduation requirements, we needed to take all the courses prescribed, which included a second language. I would need to take German. Because I had studied French in high school, not German, I was able to take the elementary German course. A good friend was not as fortunate and had to take the upper-level course and struggled throughout the year. My instructor spoke a clear German and was determined that we would all become fluent in the language. We were to spend hours in the library listening to tapes. I never did. I knew enough to get by. I would put in my time in class but would concentrate on the other subjects during study time. My instructor wasn't pleased, but I was granted a B+ at the end. I still chuckle when I recall a fellow student. We were being taught the rules of grammar, and she would ask this student why he used a certain word. He would reply that it sounded right! She was pulling her hair out!

Graduation day arrived on April 28, 1974. I was granted a Bachelor of Theology degree. I never hung that certificate in any of my offices until I hung it in my den/office back on the farm in 1995. I was proud of the achievement but didn't wish it to be a suggestion that I was better informed than others, or something like that. A bit of Mennonite humbleness, maybe. Family came to celebrate with us as well as two couples from Osler Mennonite Church in Saskatchewan. We were surprised and pleased to see them. We were scheduled to move to Osler in August in response to their call to serve as pastor. All the planning, preparing, and dreaming was taking shape! We were ready for it yet saddened to be leaving a place and experience that had been so enriching and intimate for us. We had experienced community!

That fall I attempted to continue my U of M studies by registering in a correspondence course in history. Maybe I could complete a BA. I soon gave that up, since the work in the church more than kept me busy. Other than a few courses one winter at the Lutheran seminary in Saskatoon, this ended my formal education. I was, however, committed to life-long learning.

Life as a Carpenter

I always enjoyed working with saw, hammer, and wood. My first venture was a typical boyhood hut among the maple trees north of the house. It eventually became a two-storey affair, which required gathering up a great deal of scrap lumber from all over the yard. The downstairs room had a ladder leading to the second storey. Sometime after construction, Dad was missing his handsaw and accused me of misplacing it. I looked all over but didn't find it. I insisted that I had returned it when I had finished with it. Dad wasn't so sure, so I searched some more, but with no luck. It was that fall while I was in Morden Hospital recovering from my accident that I received word that Dad had found the saw way out in the pasture where he had been fencing. I don't recall an apology but did experience redemption. After my stay at Morden, I spent time recovering in my bedroom upstairs and made an occasional trip out to the hut. It was fall, and everything looked much different than the time when I was building it.

I lost all interest in the hut early the next spring when I went out to inspect it and, to my shock and dismay, discovered the body of our dog. (Blackie?) He had been missing since early winter. We speculated that he must have been hit by a car on the road but managed to crawl back to my hut and die there. I never spent time there again. I suspect that our dog had probably been my constant companion during construction.

I did get further experience helping with the building of a machine shed in 1962. I remember the year because Elfrieda and Jake Tiessen's wedding gathering was held there. The large west doors hadn't been completed, so we hung tarps there to keep out the wind. Those years, farmers were always able to recruit neighbours to assist in the construction of farm buildings. It was a bit of a shock when we came back to the community in 1994 and found that this practice had largely ended. Luckily I didn't know this, for I recruited brothers-in-law, cousins, son, and friends to help with shingling our restored two-and-a-half-storey house, as well as erecting a bio-tech shelter for bales a few years later!

In 1966 we were on our own farm as a newly married couple and new parents. This farmyard hadn't experienced a new building in the past sixty years. We desperately needed a new granary, for the existing ones were full of holes and beyond repair. They were barely adequate for harvested grain, but there was no place for seed grain and fertilizer the next spring. I made plans for a sixteen-by-forty building with four bins. Two would hold 1,500 bushels each, and the other two would hold 1,000 bushels each. Baby Rhonda oversaw the building from her carriage when Mom Judy brought out coffee and helped with the shingling. It was finished before harvest and painted white with blue trim and shingles. I had to make some shortcuts due to finances, but it has served its purpose.

A barn was the next project. Makes me tired just to remember the energy and drive we must have had those years. The winter of 1967 was spent drawing up plans. My brother, David, had finished Grade Twelve and was available for hire the next spring and summer. He recently insisted that I helped him build the barn. An interesting example of faulty memory! I don't remember it that way! When the weather turned reasonable in early spring, we started building the truss rafters. Might as well get these done so they would be ready when the walls were up. I don't recall who was helping me at that time. Abe Thiessen, a local farmer and carpenter, helped me set up a jig that would keep a consistent pattern for the twenty-nine rafters we would build. If you're good at math, you would think we were a rafter short. No, the two on the ends weren't required to be trusses. Abe also lent me his radial arm saw that would cut accurate angles. We used eighteen or twenty foot fir two-by-eights for the main rafter and spruce two-by-fours for the supporting parts of the truss. All glued and nailed together. They would be placed four feet apart to make a 120-foot long sheep barn. We had built up a sizable flock of sheep, and the new barn should accommodate a flock of 250 ewes.

We had been using the old, badly leaning barn that had served the Stewarts, likely since the late 1800s. Cows and horses had been kept in the front part; the rest was a granary with a wooden floor and a low ceiling. The whole length was maybe sixty feet and had a loft. This had served well when grain was brought in with horse and wagon and unloaded by hand, but not so well when trucks and augers came into use. I suspect the whole building started leaning shortly after construction. Huge poles had been put in place along the east side to prop up the structure. I likely first saw the barn in the late 1940s, and the poles had been there for some time then. I'm getting a little carried away here from the story of the new barn, but I just want to justify the decision that had been made. If we were going to farm and raise sheep, the building was a necessity.

Just two more comments about the old barn. The front stable that had housed cows and horses hadn't been cleaned out for some time, maybe years. I was determined to dig out the manure, straw, and hay till I got to the base. I eventually found it and discovered a floor that consisted of large, flat rocks! Years later, when we came back to the farm, Judy used this base and planted all kinds of vegetation between these stones. A rather ambitious project and difficult to keep clean due to the numerous weed seeds that had survived there for decades. Second, what the Stewarts saved in building the poorly constructed barn, they spent on the house. This house was very well built with two-by-six walls, a nine-foot ceiling downstairs, number one cedar shingles on the roof, and a high attic. Lorne always told me, "House was built in 1905, thirty-four-by-thirty-four, number one cedar shingles!" (When restoring the house in 1994, we discovered it was thirty-four-by-thirty-two. Too late to renegotiate the price.)

Back to the new barn. The rafters were complete, and it was time to put in the crop. Dad and I were farming together, sharing machinery, though we each had our own land. I was thinking that brother David would do the field work that I normally would be doing, and I'd concentrate on getting forms built for the concrete foundation. Dave would work the discer, followed by Dad on the seed drill. That didn't last long. Dad was not impressed with the job Dave was doing. I hadn't realized that he had never done much field work before, and it wasn't that easy to learn the ways to tackle the fields and stay ahead of the drill. So I went back to the discer. Not sure what I had Dave doing for the next two to three weeks.

Back to the foundation. Most farmers were putting up pole barns for loose housing cattle those years. Cheaper and easier construction. But I opted for a proper foundation and then a stud wall. The site for the 120-foot barn had a considerable slope, so we started a little above ground level on the east end and worked west. This far end required more like a three-foot foundation to keep it level. We were using a garden hose connected to a pail filled with water—a pretty primitive levelling device, but the barn turned out to be totally level. The foundation would require a great deal of concrete, however—more than I had estimated. We built the forms from lumber from the old barn, pounded many stakes, and wired the sides together. Nothing was engineered, but I had a pretty good idea from helping neighbours with their projects of what was required. And it all held together. A large cement mixer was hired along with two tractors with buckets to deliver the mixed concrete to the forms. We had recruited a large number of people to help with this one-day project. Concrete work had to be completed in one day. I would estimate at least twenty men volunteered their time, since these types of building bees were how barns and machine sheds were built. The next week the forms came off. This lumber would later be used again for building corrals and wind breaks.

Dave and I were now on our own, and we started putting up the walls. These were eight-foot walls with two-by-four spruce studs. These would support the four-by-eight-foot plywood sheathing. I was prepared to buy ordinary plywood that would require painting. I shopped for all the lumber at Redekopp Lumber in north Winnipeg. They had a reputation for the best prices and services, including delivery. When I went in to order the plywood, the salesman showed me another option. It was plywood, but grooved and painted brown, and used on gable ends of houses. The batch he offered me had been painted in the factory with paper placed between the sheets. However, the paper had stuck to the paint, and they were unable to sell it to the people building houses in Winnipeg. He said on a barn it wouldn't be a problem. Rain and wind would eventually get rid of the paper. He offered this to me for a considerable discount, but it did amount to about $1.50 more per sheet than what I had intended to spend. I didn't waste much time deciding to take the offer. It would save a lot of painting. The barn is now over fifty years old and still in full use. The north wall is still perfect, never needed painting. The south wall is weathered due to the years of sunshine. Nowadays, people finish these buildings with painted steel. The pole barns built fifty years ago were all gone thirty years ago. (The decisions I made in the 1960s were expensive but very good in the long run.)

After the walls were up, the rafters were put in place. They all fit! Two-by-fours were nailed across the rafters to support the steel roof sheets that had been ordered. I had ordered a heavier gauge steel than what was ordinarily used. Lucky again. In 1994, our first year back on the farm, we had a devastating hail storm that totally destroyed all crops and damaged buildings. The asphalt shingles on the granary needed to be replaced, but the steel on the barn was barely dented. Later, after harvest, Dave left us at some point. The outside structure was complete, and I had several months to work inside. A lambing room, thirty-four-by-twenty-four feet, was the plan. It required insulated walls and ceiling. The lambing (bonding) pens were built. Not sure when lambing started in 1969, but I was ready and looking forward to testing the new facilities, wired for lights and heat bulbs, with water fountains and hydrants as well. Cost of the barn was around $6,000.00, including the well. A Royal Bank loan would need repayment. Trusted the price of lambs would go up a bit.

The next major project would be on our acreage south of Swift Current in 1981. I had built a two-storey tree house at Osler, and Duane had begun his carpentry career with two huts at our parsonage. The first one ... well, it was his first one. He had used a lot of nails, so when it was time to dismantle it, it took some effort. We hauled the stuff to the dump, and by that evening he'd started on a new one. Much more sophisticated with rafters, etc. He even had the know- how to wire it for a light. This was a trade that I never entered. He gained experience and was able to assist in the Swift Current project. Our acreage (four-and-a-half acres) was basically a large cement block house that had recently been restored. It had been part of a farmyard, but there was no evidence where the farm buildings had been. On three sides of our yard were wheat fields. Some distance out in the field, there remained a row of three old wooden granaries. They hadn't been used for storage for many years. I had my eye on them and eventually walked over to inspect them. There was lumber there that could be salvaged for a small hip-roofed barn I had in mind. Rhonda had some milk goats, and Michelle wanted some sheep. Duane had been promised two dairy calves by family friends back at Osler. All of these warranted a barn.

I knew the Tiessen family that owned the farmland around our place. In fact, Jake was a cousin to Elfrieda's husband, Jake, in Manitoba. I approached him about my idea. I would dismantle the bins and clear up the site for the lumber I would salvage. There was some question about what I would do with the lumber. I said I'd build a small barn. They weren't so sure how a teacher would build a decent barn, but my idea was approved. Jake, however, wanted some of the lumber. The bigger bin had decent fir studs, and he wanted those. He wanted the best part, but I agreed. I had counted what was there and was counting on there being good material in the joists under the floors. So the dismantling began. Crowbars, nail pullers, wrecking tools, gloves, blisters. Many evening hours and Saturdays saw good progress. There was good siding on the bigger bin. It was barn siding and could be painted. We even saved the shingles and hauled everything back to our yard with our small Datsun truck, stacking it next to our proposed building site. Next spring we built forms again for the foundation. I don't recall the exact size, but something like fourteen-by-eighteen feet. A small size compared to the sheep barn, but it would fit the yard. I wanted a loft for hay bales but wasn't sure how to build a loft with enough head room. I went over to Heppners', who had a full-size hip roof barn. Checking the loft, I noted that the outside walls extended higher than the loft floor. Up in the loft, there was a two-to-three-foot straight wall before the rafters started. This was great! I would design a scaled-down version of the Heppner barn.

Concrete was provided by a company called "Little Mixer." It supplied a yard of concrete at a time, and I think two loads were sufficient. Walls were built. Loft floor put in place. The granary had good tongue and groove flooring, and this was good for the loft. There would be no chaff coming from cracks in the floor above. Rafters needed to be designed. Judy and I happened to travel to Saskatoon at that time, and the kids weren't with us. Not sure what they were doing. We observed every hip-roofed barn on the way and noted many variations. We agreed that the best design had the first part of the rafter go pretty steep, and the second part up to the peak was somewhat flat and shorter than the first. That's how it was built, and it looked good.

Later in the fall shingling still hadn't been done. I was tempted to forego the cedar shingles we had saved and buy asphalt shingles. With those, we could finish in one day. Otherwise, we'd be at it for a week or more. I mentioned my options at coffee break at SCBI. Bert Esau cautiously reminded me that I had used only recycled material thus far, so I should stick with the cedar. The next week, Duane, Rhonda, and Michelle spent time on the roof with me, often shingling after dark by the light of a single bulb. We finished the barn, and the goats, sheep, and calves moved in for winter.

Ernie and Duane, recycled lumber, 1981

The next spring we painted the barn red and spray painted the roof black. Sometime that summer, Lloyd Tiessen (Jake's son) stopped by and mentioned how good the barn looked. He said, "Ernie, you missed your calling!" He had no idea how good a teacher I was! But he must have been surprised at how good a carpenter I was. I kind of speculated their talk around their table as to what kind of a shack we would build with their old granary lumber. Unfortunately, we weren't on the best terms with these neighbours. Not sure why not. But Mrs. Tiessen, when she heard we were moving back to Manitoba into the ministry, stopped by to wish us well.

A lean-to was added later to the barn. The house veranda needed fixing, and the basement needed insulation, framing, and drywalling. Always projects to tackle. After my resignation from SCBI, I built two sections of bookshelves, which we moved three times. One section is now in my den in our cabin at Creekside.

The next building project was back at Crystal City and would be by far the most ambitious to date. We moved back to the farm at the end of June 1994 and were faced with two immediate projects. We needed to build a garage and start on the renovation/restoration project on the old 1905 farmhouse. We could never settle which it was—restoring or renovating. Maybe revitalize would capture it. Our plan was to build a garage that we could live in during the winter. Friends wondered why we wouldn't rent a place in town, but we wanted to live on the farm and be close to the projects at hand. The garage (twenty-four-by-thirty-two feet) was rather straightforward. We built it mainly by ourselves, with some help putting up the manufactured rafters. The roof was partly finished when the previously mentioned hailstorm hit. Judy and I huddled next to the wall under the partly completed roof to wait out the storm. Cousins to the east of us videotaped the storm and claimed that it lasted over twenty minutes. I remember asking Judy, speaking directly into her ear, "Will it ever end?" She couldn't hear me!

After a few days of "picking up the pieces" from the storm, it was back to construction. We decided to practise putting up drywall by ourselves, as well as doing the taping. We'd been advised to practise on a smaller project before tackling the house. I'm glad we did, for we decided we'd hire others to do the house later on. I would have liked to install the drywall but realized the taper who would need to follow me would likely turn down the job. They want few seams and no gaps, and our garage hadn't worked out like that! The next spring when the drywalling crew arrived with a large truckload of drywall and carried it into the house and up the stairs, I was doubly thankful for the decision. The young crew took several hours to complete the unloading task. I would have been at it for a week. The drywall all came in four-foot-wide sheets, but the lengths varied from eight feet up to twelve or fourteen feet. Each room had been carefully measured for the correct size of sheet to eliminate as many seams as possible.

It might sound like we didn't do much construction on the house, but we did do a lot of de-construction. We had spent two summers gutting the insides and removing all the trim, doors, and two layers of lath and plaster from the outside walls. Here we discovered the quality of the construction. The outside walls were two-by-six studs that were finished on the inside with lath and plaster. But there was another layer of lath and plaster between the studs, creating two gaps of air. So someone in 1905 had cut thousands of twenty-inch pieces of lath and nailed these between the studs to create an additional air space, hopefully to aid in warmth! No cost had been spared. The plaster was still as sound as the day it was installed. It took good blows with a sledgehammer to break it up. The refuse was shovelled out of windows onto a truck and dumped into what had been a bank barn west of the house. We later buried all this after a Caterpillar we hired also had pushed the remains of the old barn into the hole. I trust that no archeologist will ever dig through this mess to try to determine how prairie people lived in the twentieth century!

The house was thoroughly gutted. All inside walls were cleared to the studding. Individual inside walls were removed, except for bearing walls. Exterior siding was removed. There were three layers of wood on the outside, counting the siding. We left the two layers and patched holes with three-quarter-inch plywood and closed in some places where windows had been. There was some rot on the bottom of walls.

The house had sunk down over time, or maybe the ground had come up. The decision had been made to move the house forward onto a new foundation. The old stone one was beyond repair, and it would have been impossible to insulate properly. We were determined to end up with a warm house, as it had been cold and drafty when we were there in the early years of our marriage. Harms Movers, from Roseisle, Manitoba, had been contracted to build the new foundation and move the house. They did excellent work. I forgot to mention earlier that the house had a brick chimney from the basement all the way through the attic, out the roof, and above the peak of the house. It must have been forty to fifty feet high. No way to move it. I worked to split it at the height of the attic floor. I chiselled away at the bricks on two sides until the chimney was only supported and balanced in the middle. Then I needed to put planks in place to support the top of the chimney that would be left in place. We liked the aesthetics of the red chimney on an old farmhouse! At least Judy did. I knew it would be a lot of work to save it. I had it well braced and supported. The remaining bricks were pounded away. We held our breath as the last blow was administered. A bit of a shudder, and the chimney settled a fraction of an inch and held. The plan had worked. About twelve feet remained. The rest needed to be carried down two flights of stairs in five-gallon pails. Then they were stacked in a pile and, a year or two later, used for a sidewalk. Harms insisted that I cover and brace the chimney above the roof before they would move the house. I did, and it survived the move.

I sat on the flat top of the house while it was being moved. I figured it wasn't very often one had a chance of catching a ride on a house! It was a short ride. I believe this move was in September. It was later than expected, but a very wet fall had delayed the moving schedule for the company. We shingled the house in October. We needed to remove the old ones first and then install new number two cedar shingles. Asphalt shingles were considered, and were much less expensive, but didn't seem to fit with an old house with a red brick chimney. Judy won this decision. Few people would understand the time it takes to shingle with cedar. One at a time. Four to eight inches wide. Nailed by hand with short shingle nails. Duane had come home to help us for a week. We also installed our wood burning outside furnace with his assistance. Some plumbing needed to be done, which he had the skill to do.

Along with Judy's brothers, Harvey and Wayne, we started on the east side of the roof. Ladders, front-end loaders, and some scaffolding were put into place. The eve of the roof was just over twenty feet from the ground, and the roof was too steep to walk on. Over the next weeks, we worked out better ways to proceed. We would remove a row of roof boards up above where we were working. Most were ten inches wide and easily removed with a nail puller without damaging them. That gave us a hand grip, but also supplies could now be handed to us from the attic inside. Much better than hauling bundles of shingles up ladders. As I mentioned, the old ones needed to be removed, black tar paper installed, and new shingles nailed in place in perfect rows. It did require a section of the roof to be open to possible rain showers. I had checked, and average rainfall for October was just over an inch. We ended up getting over five inches before we were finished. The rain washed through three floors and ended up in the basement. Luckily, no drywall had been installed. We opened the new windows and doors that had been installed, so the wind blew through and dried up the place. No damage done, but we needed to pump the water out of the basement a number of times.

The first side of roof was pretty straightforward. The others all had dormers and valleys. Shingles needed to be cut on angles, which Judy accomplished with the radial arm saw. Several fellows from our church in Mather offered to help and climbed up on the roof. Some declined to climb up onto the roof but stayed to help us from the attic floor. I was really relieved when the job was done and no injuries had been incurred. It was a good view, however. The creek had come up into flood stage with all the rain, and we could watch that while waiting for a new batch of angled shingles to arrive! Some days were too windy, so I sent the volunteer crew home. A beautiful roof, and it shed the rain! Our photo album indicates that we started on October 4, 1994, and the pictures of us on the last section are on October 20.

We had hired KM Construction from Cartwright to do the work of real carpenters. They had agreed to do the inside work of framing the new rooms, drywalling, taping, etc. over the winter months. They had started a ready-to-move house business but had time to take on this project. They agreed to use the studding that we had saved. It was good quality fir, two-by-four lumber. Not all carpenters would agree to use old lumber. We had removed all the nails. KM had already installed the windows and doors and now came back to install the white vinyl siding, which they completed before the snow came. What a smart, totally straight house greeted us all winter whenever we returned to our yard.

By spring, the inside was ready for painting, wall papering, and installation of the end-grain floorboards we had removed. The floors then needed to be sanded and varnished. A big job! Kitchen cupboards were ordered and installed. On July 31, 1995, our thirtieth wedding anniversary, we moved our bed from the garage to the master bedroom and spent our first night in the house. We hadn't slept in the house since the fall of 1972. There was still work to do.

By Christmas, the banister pieces for the staircase had all been refinished and installed. There were eighty-one spindles, and Judy had lovingly refinished each one. This staircase was the pride of the house. We recalled a time while in Saskatchewan when we had an offer from an uncle to purchase this staircase to install in a new house he was building. When I asked what he would offer, he said, "one hundred dollars." Had he offered $1,000.00, I might have been tempted. Without the staircase, the revitalizing of the house would have been incomplete! The house was now at the stage where we could proudly welcome our four children and their families home for the holidays. In the coming years, Judy stripped and refinished a lot of doors, trim, baseboards, etc. When she had a bundle done, I would install the pieces. I don't think one ever gets a project like that totally done. When we sold the farm in 2015, there were still some baseboards missing in some upstairs rooms. We had, however, created a whole new space in the attic in 2002–03. Walls and ceiling were in pine, creating a cabin effect. It proved to be a favourite space for our family and B&B guests.

There was yet to be one more project for me under the heading of carpentry. We were moving yet again! This time onto a subdivided acreage just a quarter mile from the home place. The house/cabin would be built by KM Construction, twenty years after the above build. But I would need to build an outbuilding for storage and a garage. In the fall of 2014, I undertook to salvage lumber from a granary built by my Uncle Peter. I'm not sure if my cousin Art or his son, Jeremy, offered it to me or if I inquired about it. But it was agreed that the building had served its purpose, and its removal was an issue. Oh, why me? Was I a bear for punishment, too cheap to buy new lumber, or just dedicated to recycling? Regardless of the answer, I spent a month dismantling and ended up with a trailer load of twelve-foot fir two-by-sixes and a good supply of shiplap ten-by-one-inch lumber. (This form of lumber, with lips on both sides, was common in buildings used for grain storage. No leakage happened due to the lips. Later, plywood replaced much of this kind of lumber.) This load should be enough, I estimated, to build the walls of a sixteen-by-twenty-foot (you guessed it!) hip-roofed barn. It had been hard but satisfying work. I had basically removed all the five inside bins. The rest of the building I left for Jer to take care of. The lumber was stored in our shed over winter. In spring, using the radial arm saw, I cut the two-by-sixes to a uniform twelve-foot length by cutting off both top and bottom ends that were damaged. These trimmed lengths would serve as the studs for the barn. The downstairs would have a nine-foot ceiling, and the remaining three feet would be the straight wall in the loft. Rafters would extend from there, giving good headroom.

Construction started the September long weekend of 2015. Our cabin had been moved, and we were living on our "new place." Jason and family were out for the weekend. He had wanted to help me, and over the weekend we succeeded in erecting the walls and starting on the wall boards that were placed on an angle to strengthen the structure. Duane had lent us his air nailer, and our neighbour lent us his as well, along with his air compressor. I had intended to build with my old-fashioned hammer but had broken my right wrist that spring in a tangle with a ewe. The wrist hadn't recovered its full strength and, to be honest, nailing the shiplap onto the fir studding with three-inch nails would have been difficult. Like so many changes in equipment, it would have been difficult to go back to a hammer after the first hour.

After the weekend, I basically worked on my own. I finished the walls and put in place the joists to hold the loft floor. I then designed the pattern for the hip rafters and built those on the loft floor. I put them in place with help from Judy, especially the heavier ones on the ends. I used plywood for the roof. It was difficult for one person to finish the roof, for one had to climb up and down ladders. So I hired Henry, our neighbour's sixteen-year-old son, to help me finish. He scooted around the roof like a squirrel! I could hardly keep up with him as I was cutting each piece he would need. In no time the roof was finished. I had plans all along to sheath the building with painted steel. We chose a nice barn red for the walls and grey for the roof.

I contracted with our new neighbour, Charles Friesen, to install the steel over winter as his schedule allowed. He did so and made an excellent job.

I had designed a second-storey entry into the loft, which required an outside staircase. I built this and later added a toboggan slide, which would give a good ride into the valley pasture below. The loft had room for storage but mainly was meant for extra sleeping space when several of our family came home at the same time. Kind of three-season. It wasn't insulated, but some heaters helped for the colder seasons. This space was well used this past summer when the virus called for distancing. The downstairs was for tools along with either the tractor or pickup truck.

My latest, and likely last, carpentry project was over. I never fully realized how much building I had done. I had thought of myself more as a farmer, shepherd, and pastor. Now a want-to-be, or pretend, writer!

I'd spent a great deal of time on barn construction. I had just finished reading a book Rhonda had lent me titled *The Truth about the Barn* by David Elias, a Manitoba author. It was very interesting to read alongside time spent writing this section of the story.

Thinking back to Dad's new barn with the big loft (1943–44), I thought of the way hay was moved into the loft. I've never read a pioneer description of this technique, or seen it demonstrated at the Austin Agricultural Museum. Hay was gathered on racks from the field and stored in the loft. But how? I'll try to describe it. A hay rack was taken to the hay field, pulled by a team of horses. A sling made up of ropes and cross pieces (wooden poles) was placed on the floor of the rack. The poles might have been three feet apart with enough rope to make a net. Rope from this sling was tied to each end of the rack. The rack had six-foot-high ends to which the rope was attached. Hay was then forked by hand in an even depth of maybe two to three feet. Then another sling was laid out flat on this layer of hay, followed by a third sling to make up three layers. I'm imagining some of this, for I was quite young.

When the load was full, the horses pulled the rack up to the front of the barn. The barn roof was constructed with a peak, which might have extended out about six feet on the east end. There were big doors that opened inward that served as an entrance into the loft for the slings of hay. A steel track attached to the peak of the loft extended all the way from the inside west end wall to the peak that extended outside beyond the barn at the east end. A trolley mechanism slid on this track. Part of this trolley was lowered down to the rack by a long rope, and the rope from the two ends of the first sling were brought to the middle of the rack and attached to this piece of trolley. When this was pulled up, it created a bundle.

Now, picture this. The rope in the loft that had lowered the trolley was long enough that it went up to the peak, all the way the length of the track to the far west end, around a series of pulleys and through a hole to the outside down to the far corner to ground level, where it again wound around another pulley. The horses had been unhitched from the rack. The double tree was dragged behind the horses as they were walked to the far corner of the barn, and the long rope was attached to the double tree. The double tree allowed a team of horses to pull a wagon or implement evenly. The horses started pulling. At the rack, the first bundle was drawn skyward. When the bundle reached the top, the trolley attached to the track, was pulled through the big doors and then scooted toward the west end of the loft on this track. At some point, the horses stopped and a lighter rope was pulled, which tripped the trolley and opened the sling. Hay fell to the loft floor. Somehow, the trolley and the empty sling were pulled back and down. I imagine this was done by hand and the process was repeated with the next sling. When finished, the slings were hung on the rack ends in a system that worked, and back they went to the field for the next load. It was a lot of hard work for the men in charge but sure fun to watch for a young farm kid! That rope must have been very long. It would have had to have been stored indoors to protect it from rot when not in use. When the loft was full, it provided a great place to play. No playground equipment was needed in that era.

I don't imagine a reader can easily follow, or imagine, all of this, but it sure was fun to write!

Life as a Shepherd

A shepherd with a flock can mean two things: Would one think first of a person on a farm with a number of woolly creatures, or would one think of a person with a white collar in front of a congregation? I suppose I was both, but without the collar. Our brand of Mennonites didn't wear a collar. Some Mennonite bishops in the southern USA would. One day while having coffee with several farmers in the Mather store, an older man stopped me when I was leaving and asked, "So, Ernie, which flock do you prefer?" He wasn't from my flock.

I looked around to see if any of my flock were within hearing distance. They weren't, and I replied, "When I tire of one, I go on to the other!" He laughed! There are several parallels between the two types of shepherds, but they need to be carefully stated. This chapter will be about the woolly variety.

There were several small flocks of sheep in our community when I was growing up, but these were far outnumbered by cattle and hogs. Some of the farmers who had sheep indicated there was likely more profit in sheep than any of their other enterprises. I took note of that. While I was at university studying agriculture, I encountered the subject of sheep within a course broadly called, "Livestock Management." I paid special attention to this section, and in the final semester designed a farm business plan with sheep as the livestock component. I knew that Dad would never go for this plan, but I did it just for my own curiosity. I now wish I had kept a copy of that document. I did get good marks for it.

When back home after graduation, I floated my idea of buying a small flock of sheep. Dad didn't veto this idea, even though the sheep would be kept in our farmyard with dairy cattle, a beef herd, pigs, and some chickens. A truly mixed farm, the type that was beginning to go out of style. We made contact with Mr. Calvin Foster from Mather, who was selling his flock of Suffolk sheep. These were a black-faced breed that were the most popular at the time. By the fall of 1961, I had secured a building suitable for sheep and set it up in the barnyard. Ten acres of pasture next to the barnyard was fenced with page wire, and the sheep were brought home. There were fourteen mature ewes and ten ewe lambs, if my memory is accurate. I also had to buy a registered purebred ram. I added ten more ewes that were available nearby.

Toward the end of March the next spring, the first ewe lambed on a Sunday morning. I placed the ewe and lamb in the bonding pen I had prepared and put the lamb under a heat lamp. The lamb was weak, and I tried to help it find its nourishment from its mother. I had no experience. By afternoon, not much had changed. The lamb was still not on its feet. It was weak and listless. Grandpa Harms happened to be visiting that afternoon. He'd had sheep in Russia, so I described the situation to him, and he asked me if the lamb was of normal size. I had no idea what normal was. He didn't offer to come out to the barn to take a look. By evening, the lamb had died. What a way to start in the sheep business. I left the ewe in the bonding pen overnight. The next morning, she had birthed another three lambs! Only one survived, but the ewe had perked up and licked and fed her remaining lamb. The chance of Suffolk sheep having quads was one in ten thousand. My first ewe had quads! The chance of that happening might be one in a million. The rest of the lambing went well. I likely lost some more but ended up with a decent first crop. T.S. Taylor, a Mather triplet born in 1920, and one of the friendliest people imaginable, would often remind me, "If you have livestock, you will also have deadstock." How true. Yet I never got used to finding a dead lamb or ewe and merely shrugging my shoulders. It always remained painful.

Spring was shearing season. Frank De Crane was a shearer who made his rounds doing custom shearing in our part of the province. He worked with hand shears and agreed to shear my flock, though he had no wish to add many more, since he was older and said it was time to quit. He said he would train me and the next year I would shear my own. I agreed to this, and he lent me an extra hand shear, showed me how to sharpen it, and we were on our way. It was tiring work, and I was struggling. He would finish two or three and then finish the one I had started, as I was not yet halfway finished. But he stuck with me and gave me pointers, and I would watch his procedure. He had a good policy. After shearing for a time, he would stop to relax and smoke his pipe. I later thought, while shearing, that I should have learned to smoke a pipe. It provided a reason for a break! He charged me $9.00!

The next year or two, I sheared my own by hand. I bought electric shears at some point and used those for many years, even doing some custom shearing later in Saskatchewan. I sheared for the Epps at Martensville for a few years before we moved from Osler. They had over one hundred ewes. They were our friends and treated me well, but it was back-breaking work. When we moved to Swift Current, they hired another shearer. It didn't turn out well, so they insisted I come back the next summer with our whole family to spend the May long weekend on their farm. We arrived on a Friday late afternoon and sheared into the evening. Saturday was a full day, and was I beat. Sunday was a day of rest, worship, and visiting with friends at Osler. We ended up playing soccer with the kids! Monday was finishing up the flock. The last ones were the big, heavy rams. Why leave them to the end? Well, avoid them as long as possible, and maybe we would forget about them! On the other hand, if I would start off with them, I might be too beat to continue. I must have had some speed by then to shear 120 plus sheep on a weekend. The next spring, Edgar would phone to make arrangements. I'd ask the size of the flock. He was usually somewhat evasive, knowing if he quoted too high a number, I might decline! There always ended up being more sheep than he had told me. I think we did this for three years or so. I did a bit of shearing around Swift Current as well. If I said I didn't want to travel the distance to the farm, they said they'd bring the sheep to our acreage. They only had six ewes. When they came, they admitted that the sheep had not been sheared for two years! I was relieved when the shears finally quit on me at Swift Current. Later, back at Crystal City, I needed to buy new shears, but I had a policy of no custom shearing, and never did. I did lend my shears out on occasion. That's a glimpse into the wool part of the sheep.

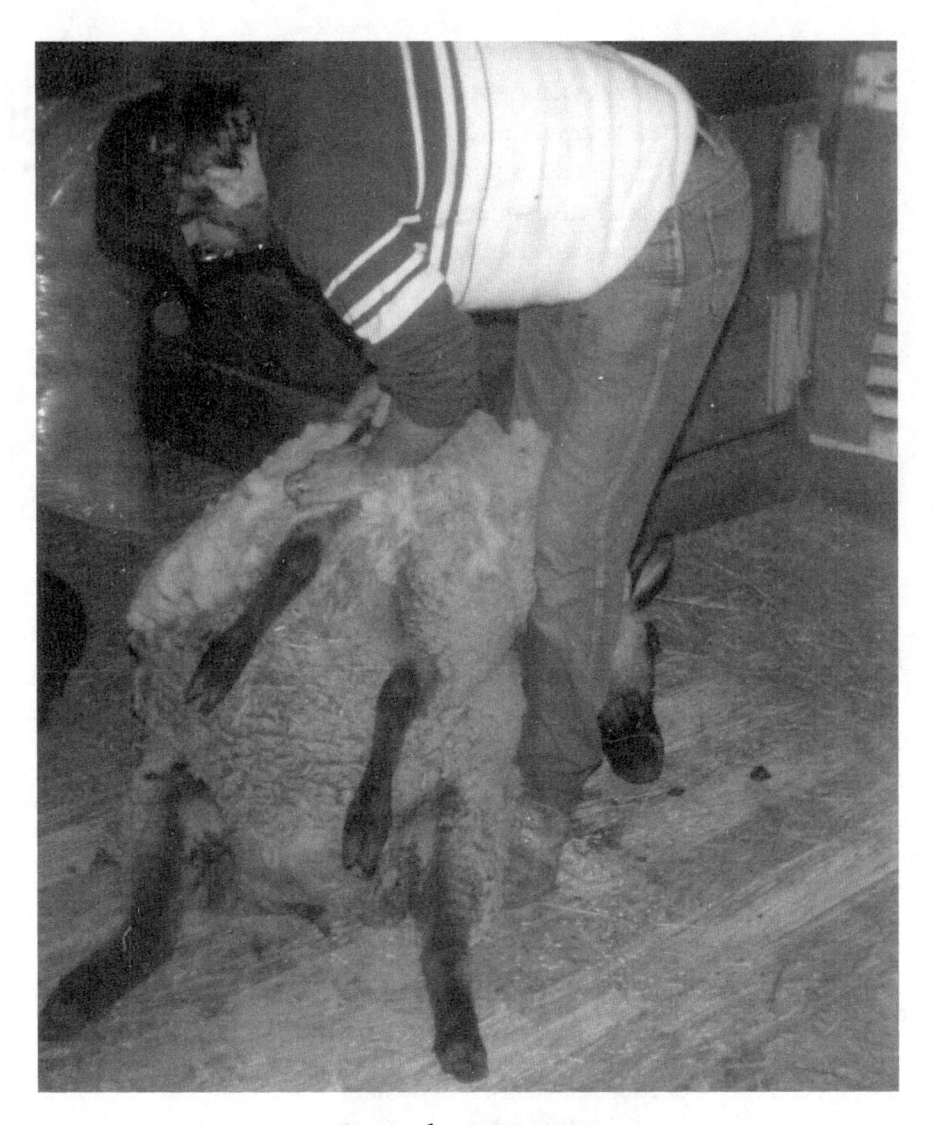

Ernie shearing, 1985

The better and more productive part was the raising of lambs. In 1964, I had purchased the neighbouring farm to the south of the home place. I spent time in the fall building page wire fences and moving my flock there for the winter. The flock had grown, and I needed more space. I used the old barn and got it ready for spring lambing. I must have walked to that place all winter to do my chores. It was just over half a mile, but there was snow in winter and mud in spring. Meanwhile, I was helping Dad with his chores. I really don't remember much of this. (I was dating Judy and was likely looking at engagement rings, so probably just going through the motions on the farm!) I have an aerial farmyard picture from the fall of 1964. The owners had moved that fall, and I had possession at that time. In the photo there are sheep in the barnyard and some feed troughs. So the sheep were there, and I wouldn't have moved them back for the winter. This was the start of sheep on this place. The flock would grow to 250 ewes, and by 1968 they'd be housed in the new barn. I had bought several flocks, but some didn't turn out that well. One fall I talked to a lamb buyer at the stock yards in St. Boniface and asked if he would select good ewe lambs for me that were being brought in to the auction. I would bring in my load of market lambs and then haul these back home. I had built a second deck on our one-ton farm truck, with extension racks, so I could load fifty lambs per trip. The buyer agreed to my proposal, so my flock grew by one hundred ewe lambs. These would be the basis of my flock in the next years. They were mainly Suffolk and were of good stock. The problem was that most ewe lambs had singles the first year, and these were usually a good size, bigger than twins. This breed, at this age, had trouble birthing on their own. I had to keep a close watch but lost too many lambs due to this reason alone. The second lambing wasn't a problem. I don't think I ever achieved a 150 per cent lambing, which was a lambing standard with this breed. But I built up a nice flock over time. When the buyer came from Ontario to buy the flock in 1971, he was generally pleased. He did cull out a number, which was expected. He wondered about one particular ewe that was on the thin side. I told him she was one of the best. She always raised twins! That's why she's thin. He took her! This was to be the first phase of my shepherding life. More was to come.

In 1994, we came back to the farm with the thought that a sheep enterprise would be one component of "making a living." We'd had a few sheep and goats on our acreage at Swift Current. These belonged to the girls and provided a great deal of fun for the family and the many guests who stopped by for a visit. However, that was not a serious economic venture. Several decisions had to be made in order to establish a new flock. I visited with a shepherd in the community who'd had a flock for many years. He was phasing out of farming but was willing to update me regarding breeds available and marketing options. Suffolk were no longer the best breed. Many options were now available that I hadn't heard of. A few months later, he informed me that a flock of Polypay ewes were available and wondered if he should buy them. He would then offer them to me the next fall. He went to look at them and decided against the purchase. However, the breed interested me. It had been developed in the United States by cross breeding four different breeds. The goal was to develop a breed with high lambing percentage, easy birthing, good mothering instincts, good milk production, superior carcass, flocking instinct, and a reasonable wool clip. This should result in a profitable flock, thus the name "poli (many offspring) pay (profitable). A creative but rather odd name!

I was being encouraged by a farmer from further west to consider emus as an option to sheep. He had a number of these (birds? herd? flock?) and was willing to sell me a number of breeding pairs. Emus, along with bison, elk, and wild boars, were being promoted as an attempt at agriculture diversification by the government. I did go to visit his ranch, more out of curiosity than a serious interest. Emus would have fit into our existing barn, but I was much more confident in sheep than learning a whole new option. I asked about potential revenue. The people in the business were only relying on the sale of breeding stock. What would happen when that market was saturated? He assured me that there would be a market for the eggs, feathers, and meat. Europeans, we were told, were very interested in the meat from emus, bison, and wild boar in their high-end restaurants. This proved not to be the case. Within a few years, emus disappeared, and the last people who purchased stock lost their investment. Wild boar also largely came to naught. Too many had escaped and truly became wild boar. They have become a serious menace in parts of the country. There are still some bison herds, but few elk. I was so glad that I decided to stick with sheep.

I noted an ad in the farm papers for Polypay ewe lambs for sale at Lumsden, Saskatchewan and called and arranged to stop by to see them on our way to Saskatoon to visit family. They looked good. It was lambing time, so I had a good view of the mothers along with the newborn. They were a white breed. No black faces and legs. It would take some getting used to. I was told I would need to decide soon, since he was getting several inquiries. We decided to order them before returning home and stopped by to make arrangements for a deposit and a pick-up in fall. We decided on sixty to start our flock. I needed to establish some corrals and upgrade the pasture fencing over the summer. We only had a half-ton truck, so I needed to rent something to haul them. I checked with my cousin, Art, to see if his truck and forty-foot livestock trailer would be available, and I offered to pay rent. He said that if I would help them with their flax harvest for a few days, the rent would be cash free. I believe he was losing his harvest help, since his sons were back in high school and university. This was a good deal for me, and also the start of assisting them in many harvests in the next years. I got to operate one of the John Deere 9400s, a self-propelled combine. I'd always longed to operate such equipment. With Dad over the years, he'd done all the combining, and I did the trucking. I had spent a few hours on such equipment both at Osler and later at Springstein. When Gerry, at Springstein, wondered if I would operate his self-propelled combine for a day one fall, he asked me if I had experience. I said yes and spent the rest of the day in the seat. When finished, I told him I now had ten hours of experience, up from the one hour of previous experience! Not sure if he was impressed or not!

Back to sheep. How one can get carried away! Earlier in the summer we had ordered two registered Polypay rams from the Balderson ranch at Magrath, Alberta. In August, we packed up our somewhat rusted Ford half-ton truck with a tool box, a few straw bales, and our suitcases in the back. Jason had the back seat, where he could stretch out for a nap! It was a multi-purpose journey. We would first stop for a few days in Calgary to attend Duane and Andrea's wedding. In fact, I was the officiating minister! I do admit I was somewhat embarrassed parking this vehicle in the lot at the hotel where we and all the out-of-town guests were staying. We made several trips to Heritage Park, where Duane and Andrea were to be wed. The wedding and reception went well. By Sunday evening, we were in Lethbridge and found a motel room for the night. Jason had caught a ride back to Manitoba with a friend. Our intention was an early Monday start to pick up the rams, but we slept in! Badly! We didn't leave the ranch until noon and had 1,300 kilometres to drive. The rams travelled well—much better than we did! It was long past midnight before we unloaded them on our farm.

We arranged to pick up the ewe lambs the first week of September. I built an upper deck on the front half of the stock trailer. I had found the same planks I had used to build the upper deck on the ton truck I had used over twenty years earlier! Some things do not disappear! The seven-hour trip to Lumsden went well. John, Rhonda, and boys met us there for supper and a trip out to see the lambs, but we couldn't get close to them due to a guard llama! The owners weren't home. Judy and I tented overnight and the next morning headed back to the farm. The lambs were sorted for loading. The owner looked at the trailer and grew upset, telling me there wasn't nearly enough space for sixty lambs. I showed him the upper deck, but he still wasn't convinced. I was confident with the space but told him that if they didn't fit, I'd come back in two days with my half-ton and pick up the remainder. They all were loaded. It was full but very manageable. At one service station, the attendant wondered what we were hauling. He could see the legs of the lambs in the upper deck and couldn't figure out what these long-legged animals could be! We got home in good time, and our starting flock was in place.

March, and the lambing season started. I had been nervous and wondered what we would experience. Was the nutrition I had supplied adequate? Would the newborn be strong? Wow, were we in for a surprise! The ewe lambs delivered their offspring easily. The lambs were vigorous and nursed soon after birth. And the numbers! These sixty ewes all lambed, and we had 108 lambs when they were finished! Over 150 per cent. Polypays were paying off! They delivered as advertised! The next few years, the percentage approached 250 per cent as the flock matured. I had been feeding the ewes extra feed two weeks before breeding. This was called "flushing" and was meant to increase the lambing percentage. I stopped this after a few years, since we were ending up with too many triplets and quads that required bottle feeding. What a problem to encounter!

Lambing time was a very busy but enjoyable time. Judy would help with chores during this season. When we went out in the morning, we would first check on new births and move them into the lambing barn. She would feed the ewes barley and then offer water to each in their individual bonding pen. A slice of my best alfalfa was next, as well as straw for bedding as required. All would then be peaceful, and she would take favourite little lambs in her arms and sit down on a straw bale and sing a lullaby! Meanwhile, I was feeding the sheep outside. A few days after the start of lambing, there would already be some mothers and lambs outside in a separate corral. The ewes still waiting to lamb were kept in the winter corral, but then switches needed to be made as numbers grew on one side and diminished on the other. It all worked, and improvisation took place over the years. The breeding flock was generally around 110 in size but grew one year to closer to 150. Mad cow disease in 2001 caused cattle and sheep prices to plummet. I had fifty very nice ewe lambs that would fetch a very poor price, so I kept them and we had a pile of lambs the next spring!

We carried on in this fashion through twenty lambings till 2015. Our flock numbers decreased the last two years with just thirty the final year. We were both over seventy years of age and were making decisions for the next chapter of our life. We could have stayed on the farm a few more years if the timing would have been different. However, we had decided to establish a new yard on an acreage instead of moving into town, and thought we better do that sooner rather than later.

A little bit more regarding shepherding. The lambing season was quite condensed, usually finished in three weeks. During that time, many trips were made across the yard. We had opted for winter lambing starting in January, as we had run into coyote problems when we had sent March/April born lambs out to pasture. Winter-born lambs would be weaned in May and kept in the corral and finished for market starting in June. Coyotes lost their menu! The ewes on pasture were safe, as the coyotes didn't tackle mature sheep. Winter lambing required extra care. The daily schedule started at 3:00 a.m., when I'd make my first trip to the barn. I got to appreciate the starry sky! If there had been no new births, I could be back in bed in twenty minutes. We had an early breakfast at 7:00. This was an adjustment. Earlier years, I would have gone out before breakfast, but I reasoned that breakfast wouldn't take that long so would save a trip. I'd go out by 7:30, check for lambs, and start the chores. Judy would join me shortly to do the "inside chores." I'd update her on the new overnight arrivals. Chores might take one to two hours. One more trip before lunch, one in the mid-afternoon, and then chores at 5:00 p.m. A trip out at 9:00 and another at midnight. These were the standard trips. If I checked and a ewe was showing early signs of lambing, I'd leave her for an hour and check again. This might require several trips. Usually, from first signs to birth would be an hour or two. If longer, I'd have to intervene and often encountered a problem. There were several different delivery problems, especially with multiple births. I was the midwife and developed a reputation and was called upon to assist other shepherds starting in the business. I estimated about 10 per cent of ewes required some form of assistance. Most were minor, maybe a leg or two twisted back, but I recall certain very difficult ones. Only one time I had to give up, and this was on a neighbour's farm. The ewe had to be put down. Not pleasant to experience.

Enough of lambing. The main market for lambs was a lamb buyer just south of Brandon. I could phone him and inquire what price he was offering, load up thirty lambs in our trailer, and be there by mid-morning. He always had a cheque ready when lambs were unloaded. Then Judy and I were off to Brandon to Joey's Only for a fish lunch and mud pie dessert. The dessert was ordered only if the lamb price had been good! With some shopping and a stop at the antique shops on the way home, some of our revenue was gone! We made many trips this way, until the buyer quit his business and we needed to find a new market. This lamb buyer had dealt with tens of thousands of sheep and lambs all over western Canada. I was just a very minor client, but he got to know me. When I was about to deposit his cheque one of the first years, I noted that the payment was almost double what I expected. Generally, it was just over $3,300.00, but this cheque was over $6,000.00! I called Roy and informed him about the amount of his payment. I said, "Roy, if this was meant as a Christmas bonus, I want to thank you!" He was quiet for some time, swore a bit (he had a colourful and crude vocabulary), and finally said he wondered how often these mistakes were made by his accountant. He asked me to tear up the cheque and he'd send me a replacement with the correct amount. I'm convinced he always remembered this experience and always treated me very well. I overlooked his language, though I know of people who resisted doing business with him for this reason alone.

The last two to three years, we sold most of our lambs through the Winnipeg Livestock Auction. We had been selling cull ewes there for some time. These were sold in early December when the price was higher. Sheep sales were held every two weeks on Thursdays. A lot of the lambs and sheep brought to this sale were small in number and not uniform in weight or quality. We'd bring in a load of thirty lambs of uniform weight and quality and often secured the highest price. We took in our last load in June 2015, with several cull ewes and the last of our lambs. I never heard it, but Judy noted that the auctioneer had informed the buyers that these were Ernie Hildebrand's lambs! We had a reputation even here, and I almost regretted the decision to retire from sheep! I suppose we ended on a high note!

Just a few details of our shearing season. I would generally start shearing as soon as the temperatures reached five to ten degrees Celsius during the day, often at the end of March or early April. The sheep were all in the corrals, so there was no rounding them up from the pasture. I'd set up in the now-empty lambing barn and bring in six to eight sheep, often with their lambs, to shear before lunch. I had bought a tipping table, which I used to trim the hooves of the sheep. The one disadvantage with this breed was the necessity for this procedure. From the tipping table I'd assist them to the shearing floor. I would shear ten to twelve per day the first days (four per hour, and Judy would bring me coffee in the afternoon) and would finish shearing up to twenty per day. I borrowed a hydraulic wool bagger to fill the big wool bags. There were still chores to do with the one hundred plus ewes and two hundred plus lambs. I always fed by hand. Small square bales and five-gallon pails for barley. It all worked, and I kept in good physical condition (which had been one of my goals in going back to farming.) At one point, I estimated I moved over two thousand pounds of feeding material per day! No gym required.

I will conclude with a story and a sermon! The story I thought might someday become a children's storybook. Maybe after this book? I had spent all winter, including the start of lambing, in my winter clothes and a bright yellow toque. The flock was a gentle one and always welcomed me when I came to feed them. During lambing, when I went for the 3:00 a.m. check, I'd lightly tap on the door into the west barn and then open the sliding door and switch on the light. All the heavily pregnant ewes would be lying down. The first nights of lambing, some would get up and move away from the door. They soon got used to my nightly appearance and all remained lying down. This made it convenient to check if any were in labour. We had a very cold spell one week, and nighttime temps dipped close to minus forty. I needed to dress more warmly. That night when I entered the door in my regular way, all the sheep were aroused and got up. I wondered if I hadn't knocked loudly enough. It was odd. The next night I made sure to knock louder, but when I turned on the light, all the sheep got up again. I pondered the mystery. Then I realized I was wearing a fur cap (made with muskrat fur) instead of my regular yellow toque. The sheep hadn't recognized me! Sheep are not as dim-witted as is often stated! Mystery solved. The weather improved, and I went back to my yellow toque!

I would occasionally listen to a sermon based on Psalm 23 (The Lord is my Shepherd) or Jesus as the good shepherd. They would be good sermons, but I would comment that the preacher knew very little about sheep! I suppose not knowing much about a subject doesn't prevent many of us from stating our opinion! I will relate one observation based on my experience. Domestic sheep and lambs definitely need a shepherd. They can get into a lot of difficulty, and it's only the shepherd that can rescue them. I might elaborate more on this later on. We people also get into a lot of difficulty, just like our woolly friends. We pray to our good shepherd and his two-legged fellow wanderers to come to our aid. We may, depending on our religious understanding, utter a prayer of thanks, but we don't acknowledge enough the ones who the good shepherd sent to actually rescue us. Ponder the mystery! Amen.

Life as a Protester

We as a family moved to Osler, Saskatchewan in August 1974 when I accepted the position as pastor of Osler Mennonite Church. I felt I had sufficient training and Christian commitment to take on this role. My intention was to be a pastor. I was prepared to lead the worship services, preach the sermons, be an educational resource, and provide pastoral care to the congregation. I was also interested in the wider community and wanted to get to know people and possibly get involved on some community committees. This was what was generally accepted as the pastor's role, accepted by pastors and congregations alike. I had committed to a three-year term and expected this would be extended if agreed upon by both parties. Neither I nor the good people of Osler were expecting that something might disrupt a rather peaceful and conflict-free ministry! We were in for a shock!

Rumours started circulating in the spring of 1976 that a major development was being proposed on a large tract of land east of Warman. Farmers were being courted to sell options on their land for a purpose not yet disclosed. Eventually the purpose was flushed out. Eldorado Nuclear, a federal crown corporation, was proposing to build a uranium refinery on the site. Due to the months of secrecy, a lot of suspicions had been aroused. There were several connections between the landowners and our church at Osler. At one point, hundreds of people who were trying to get answers gathered at Warman for a meeting. As well, several individuals were spending a lot of effort trying to get handles as to what the community was facing. I became aware of what was happening and read news reports, which included speculation as well as some facts.

I prepared to preach a sermon in Osler on September 19, 1976, entitled "A Christian Response to the Nuclear Energy Question." When I re-read this sermon now, I'm rather impressed with it! I linked the issue with our responsibility to care for the earth and the practice of stewardship. I provided a brief overview of official church statements regarding nuclear weapons and also the use of the "peaceful atom." I included a brief explanation of the nuclear cycle. I concluded with issues that were being identified, such as the use of energy and the waste of energy. There was a fear that oil had reached its peak in production and alternative energy supplies were needed. A second issue concerned alternatives to oil and nuclear—renewable sources. A third issue was the danger of the technology and the storage of waste material, which would remain a hazard for thousands of years. A fourth issue was the connection with the manufacture of bombs used in warfare. I concluded that this was not an issue solely for the landowners who were faced with their decision to sign the options on their farmland, but rather a global concern for all of us. I had stated my position, and it was received by the congregation. A meeting was arranged with the landowners that evening, and I was asked to present the message to them around a kitchen table. I could have left it at that. Preach a sermon and watch to see the impact. I ended up getting more involved, and at the end received the reputation of being a protester, and thus a troublemaker.

I don't recall if Bert Lobe (principal at Waldheim High School and former member of our church) confronted me before the sermon or after, but he asked me what we as a church were going to do about the issue. At that point I couldn't say, but eventually we arranged for a meeting in our church basement with Bill Janzen, who was head of the MCC Ottawa office. He was interested in the issue we were facing. He happened to be in the area, so we asked him to give us some information on how to dialogue with government officials. His roots were in the Saskatchewan Valley, and he was highly respected. This meeting was open to the wider community and not restricted to our church or only Mennonite people. At the end of the meeting, several people expressed willingness to proceed with the issue. These people and several others formed the first organized committee to address the concern and chose the name, "Warman & District Concerned Citizens Group." Several people who had done considerable research into the issue over the past months became members of the executive. There was also a direct connection to one of the landowners. This organization was a community group, not an exclusively church or Mennonite group, even though there was a significant Osler Church influence. I had volunteered my interest in further exploration of the issue and ended up being chosen to be the chairman at the first official meeting in late winter 1977. I was not present at that meeting, since I had some church responsibilities that evening. The citizens group, which I continued to chair, remained intact until the summer of 1980!

I won't attempt to tell the whole story, as *The Warman Story: The Refinery That Never Was* has been written by G.A. McConnell. She had access to considerable material gathered by Allan Siebert, a reporter for the Mennonite Press. Allan had envisioned a book but was unable to proceed due to health issues. MCC commissioned the book, but few copies were printed. Basically, the story was shelved due to its controversial nature. Conservative voices in MCC Canada had objected to its wider distribution. That is unfortunate, because such conservative voices in Warman and district solidly supported the resistance to the refinery. A book needs to be written to document the "coming together" of liberal and conservative voices on this issue. Also, *The Warman Story* needs to be re-issued in a more permanent form than the manuscript style in which it now exists.

It didn't take the committee long to recognize that we were facing a major issue. We knew next to nothing about the technology and were facing the forces of provincial and federal governments firmly in favour of this proposed development. We were also facing an industry with almost unlimited resources. The project was supported by the local town council and the municipal council in charge of re-zoning. Who were we? An assortment, a rather ragged group, ranging in age from seventeen to seventy. Our senior rep kept reminding us that he only had a Grade Eight education. Another member was completing her PhD in philosophy! Another was just finishing high school. We had students, teachers, administrators, business people, and one pastor. Each of us could write our own account of those three years, 1977–80. Each would be different yet would mesh together. One thing of which we reminded one another was that while we weren't experts in technology or science, we were experts in living in our community, and we were determined to have our "expertise" heard. The powers that be (the panel) would need to determine by listening to all voices.

We began as a concerned group, determined to learn all we could about all the issues and share our findings with the wider community. We took on the role of informing our community. We asked a lot of questions of politicians, scientists, and industry personnel. We met with Eldorado officials several times and got to know them by name. The vice-president of the company was among them. I recall inviting four of them to have supper with us in our parsonage before a scheduled meeting with our executive. Imagine that! Judy and I with our four children engaging in conversation around our table in our very modest home! The Three Mile Island accident in the USA had just occurred that week, and I asked if this event had an impact on their company. Their PR person quickly stated, "Absolutely not!" He spoke too soon. He was corrected by another, who indicated it had created a pause, but they had concluded that they still had faith in the safety of their industry. That evening, our rag-tag group met with these people dressed in suits. We were quite intimidated, but we came prepared to ask our questions. This questioning technique (we hadn't deliberately chosen this style; we just wanted to know) proved to be very effective. We asked why the company needed nine quarters of land for a refinery that required only twenty to thirty acres if the refinery was totally safe. We asked about the plan to store the two thousand tons of annual waste on the site. Above ground initially, in steel drums, we were told, and then several hundred feet below ground. What about ground water contamination in that case? Would it affect drinking water in the area and the many dairy herds? We were told the company would need to experiment. We questioned the connection with the arms race, knowing that Canadian uranium was a component in the bombs used in World War Two. We found out that evening that they couldn't re-assure us. Their responses were feeble. Eldorado preferred to conduct public information meetings with a full display of charts outlining the nuclear cycle and all the benefits of the power generated. They were not prepared for vigorous debate with people already somewhat informed.

We had experienced an early version of the next few years' dynamics. The president of the company had made a statement that they would not build the refinery in a community that didn't want them. How that was to be determined was unclear. We were well on our way as concerned citizens. By the time of the hearings, we had determined that we were opposed to the refinery being built anywhere. We had grave reservations about the whole nuclear cycle and felt uranium would be best kept in the ground. We would have support for this position from the indigenous community. Their people had, centuries earlier, sensed that places that held deposits were to be avoided and deemed them "holy places." Modern commerce was scattering this material all over the face of the earth. This begs the question, "Where is wisdom to be found?"

Three weeks of hearings before a federally appointed environmental committee began in January 1980. Our group's membership surpassed eight hundred by this point. People from all walks of life came to speak. We had been encouraged to come and voice our opinion and had been told that all who came would be heard. The panel hadn't been prepared for the response. Experts, because they lived in the community (from thirteen-year-olds to German-speaking grandmothers and all in between), pitted against experts in science, industry, economic development, and government. It seemed totally unfair: the outside experts with available funds in the millions to conduct the hearings against us, who had spent years as volunteers with no reimbursement even for travel. We did get a grant of $13,000 delivered the first week of the hearing, which we used to reimburse people from outside our province who provided some of the expertise we lacked. We had been encouraged to hire a young environmental lawyer from Saskatoon, as we might need to fight in court in the future. I didn't favour this direction. How would we ever finance a court battle? I was prepared for the panel to make their decision and then abide by it. However, others differed in opinion, and we hired the lawyer. He submitted his first invoice to our committee after meeting with us a few times. He documented time spent in each phone call, every mile travelled, and the hourly rate for his time in travel and consulting with us. He submitted this bill to us, who had no bank account and had spent three years of time and thousands of miles travelled with no reimbursement! We had to decline further services! Thankfully, we would get the grant and be able to pay his bill.

The hearing ended. Transcripts filled many boxes. Anxious waiting took place. The deadline for reporting on the panel's conclusions was extended several times. In August, the final report was issued. The panel determined that the refinery process itself was acceptable, but Eldorado had failed to properly assess the social situation. They could do a further study of the people residing in the area and submit to another hearing or choose another site. After some consideration, they abandoned this site and eventually abandoned Saskatchewan. They never did build another refinery.

Some random thoughts and memories. In the second year of dealing with the issue, I was filling up our car at the local Texaco station and went in to pay for the purchase. I was told I had credit on account. When I asked how this was possible, they explained that a local farmer had made a payment and credited me for several tanks of gas. I was told who he was—one of our older dairy farmers from our congregation. When I met him later, I thanked him for his gift and he said, "I support what you're doing and know you make many trips to meetings. I don't go to meetings and can't help in that way. This is the least I can do." He was one of "the quiet in the land" with deep convictions! Eldorado officials never met him!

We had a neighbour family while living on a farmyard during our last year at Osler. The family, who belonged to one of the more conservative churches in the area, did not feel comfortable confronting governments and their policies. But we found out they were fully aware of the dynamics in the community and totally supported our efforts. The hearings were being broadcast on a university radio outlet, and families were following the debates "religiously!" The mother and some of her older children would come to our place some evenings to watch the Saskatchewan TV news to capture more fully what they were hearing on the radio. We understood this interest among their people was widespread and likely accounted for a large proportion of our membership. These people wouldn't be heard by the panel, and Eldorado was likely not even aware of their existence. We were being made aware that we were speaking for many people who appreciated what we were saying as well as the way we were presenting ourselves. This community would be the one to provide and serve the "faspa" when the celebration was held late that fall in the Osler school gym.

It had truly been an epic battle of David versus Goliath. As is stated in sports circles when assessing a team's chance of winning—on paper we had no chance. No one would have given us odds of winning. I wonder how we persevered in giving leadership to this issue. I suppose we wanted to be heard. If the panel would rule in Eldorado's favour, we could say we gave it a good battle. We had stuck up for our community. Forty years later, I'm still amazed when I think of that time. We had hoped to have some kind of a gathering in the summer of 2020 to mark the forty-year anniversary, but the Covid-19 virus prevented that from happening.

Forty years also allows one to consider the case we made against the uranium industry. In 1977, we were reassured a permanent disposal site for nuclear waste would be established in ten years. I checked online information on this issue and discovered it is still ten years in the future. In the 1970s discussion, over one hundred nuclear reactors would be built in Canada in the coming years. I don't think any have been built. At the hearings at Warman, the mayor of Uranium City touted what a great corporate citizen Eldorado was in their community. Within a few years, Eldorado closed the mine in that community, and the city is now close to a ghost town. We were also reassured that the proliferation of nuclear weapons was under control. I don't think anyone would assess the situation in 2020 as being under control. Oil was running out of supply in the 1970s, and renewable sources weren't feasible. Nuclear energy was needed, we were told, as a gap between oil and renewables. We have not yet reached the peak in oil production, even though demand is decreasing. Wind turbines and solar panel systems are readily seen as one travels the highways of our country. Nuclear energy was viewed as a clean energy source, which it is when compared to fossil fuels. But it contaminates the earth in a whole different way. Imagine people on this planet still needing to safeguard the wastes from this industry thousands of years in the future! What will those people say about the irresponsibility of the twentieth century?

We were a protest movement. I, along with all the others, was protesting the entry into our community of an alien industry. This protest was widespread in our province. We had support from "anti-nukes" from all over the province. The NDP government was threatened by this protest, for they realized that their core voters were among these protesters. I firmly believe, however, that it was the concentrated community at Warman & District, the Mennonite presence, undergirded by its firm faith position, that convinced the panel to reject the site. Another community without such a presence would be hard pressed to mount the opposition we were able to do. Mennonites and others—protesters!

"Protest" has a negative connotation in many circles. Farmers don't like protests that disrupt rail traffic and the movement of grain to market. "Get a job" is a common response when one views protesters on the streets on the evening news. Yet peaceful protest is allowed in our form of government and society. When we feel strongly about an issue, or a direction we believe is the wrong path, do we just sit back and say and do nothing? When we're told the decisions have already been made and that our voices will accomplish nothing, do we remain silent? We chose another option. We chose peaceful protest. But protest is costly. It causes division. We all have some scars from our involvement.

I possibly shouldn't have written this chapter, at least not framed it as protesting. Yet it does help me understand the people and their protests happening all over. I have continued to protest. I protest income taxes that finance wars and the preparation of wars. For several years I diverted the military proportion of my income taxes to Conscience Canada. These diverted funds would eventually be used for peaceful purposes. This was an act of conscientious objection to me paying for war. More recently, we increased our charitable giving and thereby reduced the amount of income taxes we would pay. I write letters to prime ministers protesting the military-industrial complex of weapons production supported by government policy and subsidies to support employment. These are complex issues that I won't pretend to fully understand. However, I do understand that in times of war there are immediate shortages of food, safe housing, schools, and jobs, but it's rare that the supply of weapons runs out. There are always more bullets and bombs in supply. Thus, I continue to protest. I also try to maintain a balance. I applaud the good in life. There is much to celebrate, and I don't view myself as only a person opposed to things!

Journey of Faith

I have documented much of my life thus far. I have covered some of the decisions that have been made along the way, activities in which I've been involved in the different places we've lived. These may well be considered the physical aspects of my life. Meanwhile, there is a parallel journey that I'll refer to as faith. It's more the inner journey of one's thoughts, feelings, and beliefs that become the basis for the life decisions one makes. At least, that's the way I conceive of it. My orientation in faith was formed in the womb of the Christian faith in the Mennonite perspective. Our extended family always belonged in the Mennonite Church and community. In my early years, this was a very isolated community with little interaction with surrounding faith traditions. This was to change dramatically in the next decades. The walls were to come down.

My earliest memory was when I was to start Sunday school. I was told by my sister and older cousins that I would need to memorize a scripture verse every week. I was apprehensive about this information, not even knowing at the time that I had a serious deficiency with the ability to memorize. The first verse was, "Gott ist die Liebe." (God is love.) That's easy, I thought! I fully agreed with the verse, since early lessons from my mother and the saying of prayers fully informed me that God was love. I saw myself as wanting to live a godly life.

Sunday school proceeded. Often as a new year started, we would start with Genesis 1 and learn the early Old Testament stories. I questioned the story of the fall. I asked my teacher what the serpent must have looked like before God cursed him to henceforth crawl on his belly. Did he have a series of legs to support his long body? (I would have asked this in German but have no idea how to say that today!) I don't recall the response from the teacher but I remember feeling a little pride in asking the question. Teachers must dread such students!

Some years later, I was startled one Sunday morning. My Uncle Abram usually led the opening of all the classes with singing, prayer, and a brief meditation. He was a kind and gentle educator of children. A new, very talented woman had moved into our community and led the beginning of the classes that Sunday. She asked us a question: "How many of you have been saved?" I was in shock. I had never heard that kind of question before. What did it mean? Was there another expectation that God had of us beyond loving him? Not one person responded to the question. There was utter silence. She shook her head and said, "That's so sad. Not one of you is saved." This would affect me for years to follow. This experience suggested to me that there was another requirement to fulfill, but there was no avenue to do this. In reflection in later years, I believe if she would have led us in a prayer asking for forgiveness and committing ourselves to follow Jesus, we would all have responded in agreement and could have been pronounced saved.

It wasn't until I was in Winnipeg in 1959 and attended a large evangelistic rally with a well-known American preacher that I met this requirement. I went to the "front" to signal my intention and was counselled further after the service. My counsellor was a CMBC student who later became a pastor. I really didn't need this session. I knew everything that he was telling me; after all, I always went to church. I had just gone "forward" to fulfill what I conceived to be a requirement. I met this man at a retired pastors event recently and we talked about the dynamics of those type of events. It was just part of the system at the time in Mennonite and Evangelical circles. Billy Graham was a force! (He wasn't the preacher referred to above.)

I recall some years later questioning the atonement, even though I wasn't aware I was questioning a major church doctrine. I wondered why God demanded the death of Jesus to appease him of all the human sin. Why couldn't God just declare, with a booming voice from above, "You are all forgiven!!" Imagine my surprise when I was reading one of Marcus Borg's books decades later, and he related an almost identical questioning during his youth. He was a biblical scholar and author who had grown up in North Dakota in a Lutheran Church, not one hundred miles from my home in Manitoba. He was born just a few years before I was. Regrettably, he passed away a few years ago. He had so much more to offer the faith community.

I came home from my two years in Winnipeg with new confidence. I enrolled in church membership classes (catechism) and was baptized as an adult believer in the Mennonite tradition. I became involved in youth leadership and in teaching Sunday school to a large group of high school fellows. I was learning along the way and was intrigued with the educational material provided by our North American Conference structures.

The Vietnamese war was often a topic for discussion in the context of war and peace issues. I was also elected along with two others to do some preaching in the worship services. I was feeling my way and found it to be a struggle. In order to teach and preach (to verbalize), one had to form one's thoughts and beliefs in one's own mind. A nagging thought had to do with this whole matter of being Mennonite. I knew it meant a life of non-violence and non-participation in war, but what was the basis of this distinction from the other faith traditions in our community? (I recall that an obvious distinction between Mennonite kids and the "English" kids in school was swearing. We had been brought up to never use such language. There was a fellow town student who would, when angry, swear a blue streak. I could hardly believe the words he would utter! Later, I found out that he taught Sunday school in the local United Church! It's interesting what one remembers and how one went about processing these experiences. Nowadays, some of us Mennonites also use some of these "bad" words. Not in anger necessarily, just for added emphasis!)

A remarkable event for me happened at an evening service when Rev. Allan Churchill had been asked to speak in our church. He was pastor in the United Churches in the neighbouring communities of Cartwright and Mather and became a hero of sorts to many people. He had been an RCMP officer when he experienced a dramatic call to train in pastoral ministry. After years of study in England, his first placement was in this part of Manitoba. He told us this dramatic story. A small number of his graduating class at seminary, along with their spouses, had been invited for a final meal and discussion with one of the leading faculty members. The spouses were called upon to say a little about themselves. When Allan's wife, Helen, introduced herself, she said she was a Mennonite from southern Manitoba. When asked by the professor to elaborate, she told him that Mennonites evolved from the Anabaptist Reformation of the sixteenth century. Anabaptists believed in following Jesus in life, the church was a fellowship of believers, and adherents were dedicated to the way of peace. The professor gave this some thought, took another puff on his pipe, and said, "Here I've been an Anabaptist all my life, and I didn't know it!" This story finally gave me an identity. I'm a Mennonite Anabaptist, and here was a brief capsule of what it meant! This I could build upon. I later had a visit with Rev. Churchill in his home. I wanted to hear more about how he had experienced his call, since I was also being nudged in that direction.

As documented earlier, we made the decision on our vocational change and decided on three years of theological training. One of our lay leaders wondered why I didn't go directly into pastoral work, believing I could find a position. Training was not yet a prerequisite in many of our rural churches. He questioned my plan to spend three years studying instead of immediately starting to "serve the Lord." But I wouldn't hear of this suggestion. I might have known little, but I did know this much, and it was that I didn't know nearly enough to engage in pastoral work without more training! Three years of scholastic study in history, Bible, and theology! I was beginning to grasp the enormity of knowledge available. I had a start. Enough, I thought, to be a pastor, and I could learn more along the way. I had matured in my understanding and was prepared to be a shepherd in guiding my congregation in the continuing challenge of faithfully living out our understanding of what it meant to be Christian in the twentieth century. Little did I know that this would be severely tested by the issue of the refinery and the whole matter of nuclear technology within a few years.

Within preaching, I began to stretch beyond standard assumptions. In one sermon, I challenged the common understanding of the separation of activities considered to be sacred and others as secular. I suggested that the plowing of the fields and planting of grain could be viewed as sacred activities when conducted as stewards of God's creation and the feeding of people. A church committee, on the other hand, which resorted to anger and hostility over divergent views wouldn't be seen as sacred in its behaviour at all! Another time I was on a pulpit exchange and spoke on the theme of the value God sees in our human lives. I used the slogan, "God don't make no junk!" A woman came up to me after the service with tears in her eyes, telling me she had thus far in her church experience never heard such a positive message. She had only heard how unworthy we were in our sinning ways. In another congregation at another time, a young man was coming to church occasionally. He was from a very conservative church and was courting a young woman from our community. I wondered what he was experiencing while in our midst. His future father-in-law shared with me this young man's observation. At the dinner table after a service, he had said, "I don't know what's happening to me. Normally after church I feel really bad about myself. After service here, I feel good about myself!" Recalling these events reminds me that I didn't ever advocate the doctrine of the total depravity of the human condition. While I fully acknowledge the potential evil as well as the good tendencies of human behaviour, I was seeing little merit in mainly dwelling on the negative.

A major alignment of my faith understanding was to take shape when I was past middle age. A friend from Osler introduced me to the writing of John Spong. I had heard of him before. He was a person the conservative church press warned people about. I read his books, starting with *Rescuing the Bible from Fundamentalism* and *Liberating the Gospels*. Sometime later, a son-in-law, my cousin, and I motored to Saskatchewan to listen to Spong's lectures for a weekend. The United Church of Canada sponsored this event. After the event, one of the organizers told me that they were always nervous when they had people attending from the Mennonite Church! They wondered if we would be antagonistic toward the sessions. We weren't! It was a very formative event and did nothing to discourage me from pursuing this path.

Spong's books and lectures, and books by Marcus Borg, provided a renewed view of the Christian gospel. It was becoming understood that the church was undergoing a major reformation. These events, I came to understand, happened every five hundred years or so. I had read and taught about the sixteenth century Reformation, so I had some idea about the shake up we might be facing. One can, however, only come to understand reformation in retrospect, so it's way too early to analyze what's happening. What I came to understand was that we have the traditional version of faith and now an emerging version. Few denominations are exempt from this. Most denominations and congregations have adherents of both versions. The emerging version recognizes scholarship that has been taking place for a century or more. A literal view of scripture is no longer adequate. The holy scriptures are viewed as sacred writing from two spiritual communities—the Hebrew community and the early Christian community. They are special and have much to say to us in our time but are limited in addressing issues we face today. They weren't delivered directly from above, with little input from human authors. We cannot discard the advances in scientific knowledge and separate faith and science. (I'm puzzled by voices who indicate that evolution is just not believable and prefer to believe that God, as Creator, could bring all this to being by "snapping his fingers" in six successive literal days!)

These issues are very involved and impossible to summarize, so I'm just giving a brief indication of my further faith journey. The sixteenth century had been a battle between tradition and scripture, as to which is a guide to faith. I concluded that both were a guide and then added John Wesley's teaching that "reason" was also necessary. I readily agreed with Wesley, since I recognized that I had always valued human reason. There was an expression that one didn't wish to "kiss one's brains goodbye" at the church door! So I advocate that we need another testament to add to our scriptures. We need a supplement to the two we have in the sacred scriptures. I believe that present day teachers and preachers are unofficially using what might be in this "newer testament." I don't realistically see writing added to the canon, but we need to acknowledge that we're using all sorts of knowledge to guide people in faithful living. There has been an explosion of knowledge in the past centuries. To deny this and only rely on writings from before the second century AD is unrealistic and inadequate to understanding our life, let alone God, at this time we live in.

In my first year of retirement from life as a shepherd (2015), I picked up a book in the church library. The title was *The Naked Now*, by Richard Rohr. The book cover indicated it was a book about mysticism. That term almost made me leave the book there, but I reasoned (See, I told you I used reason!) that the book had been placed there by our pastor, whom I respected greatly. And I thought that I should read something out of my comfort zone. Now, six years later, I read daily online meditations by Rohr! I'll never pretend that I understand much of what he says, but my eyes (and heart) have been opened to another understanding. I now proclaim that tradition, scripture, reason, and a mystical spirit can guide us in the emerging version of faith.

Mysticism for me opens up the elements of wonder, awe, and mystery of all that surrounds us. We watch sunrises from our breakfast table and sunsets in the evening. Toward the end of December, the sun rises over the Hudson farmstead over a mile away to the southeast. We take note of the time. Now in mid January, the sunrise has moved back north beyond the trees of this abandoned yard. The sun rises a few minutes earlier. We imagine the change of tilt of our planet. At the same time the earth is rotating and also travelling around the sun at something like two thousand miles an hour! Not sure if that's correct. I read something like that in the book by Bryson, *A Brief History of Almost Everything*. Awe and wonder! I look at nature in a new way. God is in everything, the mystics proclaim! Indigenous people speak of Mother Earth. How true. All life comes from the earth. I was born in a house in Crystal City, as there was no local hospital at the time. I was likely conceived in the home of my parents, less than a mile from where we now live. All my growth in the womb and since then has required nutrients that come from the earth, the soil. With the mystics I'd say from God. With indigenous neighbours, I'd say from Mother Earth. In death, my body will be committed, "earth to earth, ashes to ashes, dust to dust." I've spoken those words many times at grave sites. So I proclaim that I came from God (the earth) and in death I return to God (the earth). I'm satisfied with that. I trust I'll face death with this peace!

Mysticism has prompted me to review the nature of the shepherd. My forty years of experience with sheep cause me to conclude that domestic sheep really need a shepherd. Sheep and lambs can get into a lot of trouble. Adult sheep who are pregnant, and with a year's growth of wool, can lose their balance and end up on their back if they lie down on an uneven space. When this happens, they can't get back on their feet. It's up to the shepherd to push them over. They will then stagger for a while, depending on how long they were on their back, but are generally Okay. Lambs are very inquisitive. They like to jump up on things, especially bales. If there's baler twine hanging in a loop, they can get it around their neck and often strangle to death. A shepherd learns to "lamb proof" the barn and corrals, not unlike the way we child proof a house when our kids learn to crawl and will open every drawer. I've never observed a sheep assisting a fellow sheep requiring help! In fact, one day I experienced the opposite. A lamb was in trouble, and its cousins and stepbrothers and sisters were adding to its distress. The lambs had knocked over a heavy plywood panel that I used as a door to keep sheep in the barn on cold winter nights. During the day, I'd lean it against the wall. Now it had been knocked down on the floor, and a lamb was trapped underneath it. That was bad enough, but a number of lambs were lying on the panel, adding to the weight. I was angry and chased them off. Then I lifted the panel and saw the lamb. It was flat—almost like a pancake—but still alive! I helped it to its feet, and after a while it could stand on its own. Later that day, it was almost back to normal. Sheep and lambs need a shepherd. They can get into a lot of trouble. I won't even mention the shepherd's work as a midwife during lambing.

People also get into trouble. No one would argue with that. We also need shepherding. A favourite psalm in the Bible speaks of the Good Shepherd who will guide and keep one safe. This image of God is a much better one than the ones earlier writers used to describe God. There are images of God threatening death to anyone who merely touched items in his temple without authorization! The image of a Good Shepherd is a comforting image that has helped many people in distress. What happens in reality, however, is that two-legged shepherds or angels, who might be neighbours or even strangers, come to our assistance when we're in trouble. We have the exceptional stories, such as the story of the trapped miners in Chile in 2010. These miners no doubt prayed to God for rescue, but it was engineers and other specialists who came from around the globe and designed methods of rescue. These human shepherds were successful, praise God! Are we meant to be each others' shepherds? Isn't this how life is being experienced? Mysticism would credit God within the engineers with the success. Awe and wonder, mystery!

I wondered more recently if my sheep recognized me as their shepherd. What role would they understand me playing? Did the ewes worry at night as they felt their first contractions if a shepherd would be there on time if they got into trouble delivering their twins or triplets? I rather doubt it. We're beginning to recognize more the intelligence of animals, but there's a limit. I preached a sermon on this in my retirement. I asked if there was a possibility that we humans are still too dim witted (an accusation against sheep) to recognize the heavenly shepherd guarding us. Some blank stares, but a doubtful shaking of heads.

This is my journey of faith. I'm still in the church. There are pastors who lost their faith when they could no longer preach the literal understanding of faith. They failed to discover an alternative to that version. This is an occupational hazard when one takes seriously the scholarship that has taken place. My story is not a comprehensive defence of the emerging version of faith, rather only my path as I experienced it. I respect other paths. All of us should continue with utter humility. I believe it's better to respect a wide diversity of experience. Truth isn't restricted to one tradition or to any one religion. Jesus is said to have referred to the "narrow path," but I understand now that that path is the path of love and peace, not the path of any set of doctrinal beliefs. I conclude!

Life in Retirement

Stage One, 2002–2015

One of the first major projects in this stage of retirement was to renovate the attic space in our house. It was a large room with a high ceiling, which we envisioned as a great space for B&B guests and family celebrations as well. It would have a bathroom and hot tub and would accommodate larger group experiences. The attic with dormers on three sides had a complicated roof design, making it more difficult to work with. This feature, however, made for a much more interesting space. We hired our nephew, Garth, to install new windows as well as a skylight. I went to work replacing the floor. Judy had found a supply of identical flooring that had been reclaimed from a house being dismantled in town. That was the winter project. The next year, we planned to finish the sloping walls and ceiling by installing knotty pine boards throughout to create a cabin feeling.

In June, when I was golfing at a fundraising event, I was teamed up in a foursome that included Henry from Winnipeg. He was the person who had convinced us to restore the house instead of dismantling it. That had been eight years earlier. During our match, I told him that he might be interested in knowing that we were working at the attic. He just looked at me and made no comment. I thought that a bit odd but didn't say anything. Partway through the first nine holes, he responded. He reminded me that eight years ago he had offered us a week's free labour if we would proceed with restoring the house. However, he hadn't been able to do that because he had been involved in his own major house build. Now he was prepared to fulfill his promise. I was shocked! I told him I had totally forgotten about his offer and hadn't mentioned the attic project now in order to secure his free labour! He asked for advance notice and said he'd come for a week. He came and teamed up with Garth, getting most of the pine installed in five days. I was well trained by then and was able to finish the job. By Christmas 2003, the attic was complete and even decorated with a tree and other holiday trim. Our family came home, and we enjoyed this large space that was so well suited for such an occasion. Two futons provided couches during the day and beds at night. The little kids enjoyed finding a place under the eaves for their mattresses and sleeping bags. This space would also be utilized by a wide variety of B&B guests over the next eleven years!

Judy and I had hopes to do some travelling in the next years. Previously, we had joined Jason and Katharina on a trip to Germany in the spring of 2002. This was relatively inexpensive, since her family had issued an invitation for us to stay with them. Because we'd be there for two weeks, Jason wondered if we wanted to take a side trip for a few days to tour and give her family a break. Not taking long to respond, I asked if a trip to Zurich, Switzerland would be an option. I hadn't consulted any maps and was unsure of distances involved. It would be no problem. For lodging, we contacted a couple listed in the Mennonite-Your-Way directory who lived close to Zurich. I thought it would be a day's journey from our location in Germany to Zurich, but we left mid-afternoon and were there by early evening. European countries are all quite close to each other, especially when compared to Canada!

The next day in Zurich was a great experience for me. I had studied and later taught about the early years of the Anabaptist Reformation, which was centred around this city. I had never thought that I'd walk along the Limmat River where Felix Manz was drowned by the established church authorities. He was the first martyr of this Reformation, with many more to follow. We found our way to a remote cave high above the city in the Alps. Here the new adherents to Anabaptism met in secret for worship and fellowship. This site was a "must-see" for Mennonite tourists in Switzerland. This trip remains a highlight for me. The faith connection was very powerful, and the beautiful Swiss countryside was breathtaking!

The travel plans to explore Canada were, however, put on hold for a few years. We were on a pretty strict budget for the next five years, since we no longer had employment income. I was receiving Canada Pension Plan benefits, but I wouldn't receive Old Age Security until I was sixty-five. In the summer of 2003, Mad Cow disease (BSE) hit the Canadian cattle herd, and beef prices collapsed. Lamb prices also nose-dived, since the American border was closed, cutting off our export market. The lambs we shipped in June sold for $1.15 per pound. In fall, the price had dropped to sixty cents per pound. Also, there was no market for ewe lambs, which I had been selling to farmers who were wishing to start a flock or expand their flock. I had sixty great-looking ewe lambs that I didn't want to sell for slaughter, so I kept them and ended up with a greatly expanded flock myself. The prices didn't recover until 2005 but have been steady ever since.

Trips started in 2005 on an annual basis. We covered Canada from the Maritime provinces to Vancouver Island, and we made several overseas trips. We returned once more to Germany and toured into Northern Italy as well. We visited Dave and Romaine in Australia, and together with them, enjoyed a car trip around Tasmania. We booked a bus tour and travelled through England and Scotland, ending that journey with a week-long walking tour of the Cotswold Hills. Judy wanted to walk through sheep pastures in England and practised for this journey by walking through our own sheep pastures at home! It was a really unique and enjoyable experience. Sure a change of pace after spending the previous week with forty others on the bus tour! However, during this whole trip, our minds were often in a hospital room in Winnipeg. Our one-year-old granddaughter, Johanna, was awaiting surgery due to kidney cancer. The surgery wouldn't take place for some time, but her condition was serious. We had considered cancelling our trip but had been urged by family to go. There was strong support for the family at present, including her other grandmother from Germany. We would be called upon again when we came back. It was a slow recovery of many months, but today she is as healthy as any other child her age!

We also toured a few times in the USA. We enjoyed the Rockies of western Montana, and for a change of pace we visited the Amish country in Pennsylvania. Almost all of these trips from 2005 to 2014 took place in October. Before we would leave, we needed to complete the third cut of alfalfa, clean out the corrals by spreading the previous winter's manure on the alfalfa fields, prepare the corrals for winter, and dig the spuds. (We usually say "dig" when a better term is to "lift the spuds.") The Thanksgiving weekend was usually when many of our family would come home. The western families often found Thanksgiving more suitable for this trip than Christmas. Two or three days after this event, our car was packed, and we were off for two weeks or so!

Changes took place in our family during these thirteen years. We joined with Jason and Katharina when they celebrated their commitment to each other at Hope Church in Winnipeg. Their reception was held on a farmyard on the edge of the Whiteshell. Her family from Germany were able to come for this occasion. The next afternoon, rafting on huge tubes over the rapids of the Whitewood River was enjoyed by many! Six grandchildren would join our family during this time period. However, we were also losing our own parents. Judy's dad had passed away in 2001, and my parents died a few years later, both having reached ninety years of age. It had been good for us to be closer to all of them in their last decades of life. Judy's mom would outlive the others, reaching almost ninety-six years of age. That was remarkable, since she had experienced so many health issues during her lifetime. She managed to live independently right until the last few months.

Some of my friends wondered how I would fill my time after retiring from pastoral work, which had been a two-thirds time position. I replied, "I had been farming on a one-third basis. If I now work at farming at half-speed, that will fill two-thirds of my time. So I only have to fill in a bit!" I did this by continuing volunteer work on the local hospital board. In total, I served on the board for eighteen years, with seven of those years as chair. Board meetings were held monthly. and with the various committees, I probably averaged three to four meetings per month. The Health District initiated the building of an Alternative Care Unit at Prairie View Lodge in Pilot Mound during this time. The project was a total community effort, with all the funding being raised locally. My ability to hear had diminished, so eventually I needed to decline further involvement on this board. I could no longer follow the discussion around the table. I had purchased hearing aids earlier, but these aren't very helpful in larger group meetings. As my audiologist often reminded me, they are hearing aids. They aid in hearing, but they don't replace good ears!

Winters tended to be busy enough. I enjoyed more time to read and have read hundreds of novels, as well as a mixture of more serious books, like *The History of God* and *A Brief History of Nearly Everything*. Lambing season was also more relaxed, for I could concentrate on that work alone and not need to juggle other responsibilities. I also seriously re-entered the curling community. I had curled in earlier years and always enjoyed the sport. During the years at Swift Current and Springstein, there were few opportunities to curl. Judy and I did join a mixed couples league for the first years back at the farm, but that league folded after a while. There was a seniors' league that curled in the afternoons that I joined. This became a very enjoyable time for me. The old rink at Pilot Mound had been closed, so the Pilot Mound Club joined with the Crystal City Club to curl on our four-sheet rink. It was great to see thirty-two senior men and women out on the ice at a time! One skip was eighty something years old and five foot nothing tall. She was one of the best skips! I had to re-learn some of the skills of my earlier years, but I played the third position. It's a bit of a joke in curling circles that a newcomer to the sport says he will throw his rocks last, since he wants to observe how it's done. He doesn't realize that the most skilled player throws the last rocks! (But it doesn't take them long to catch on!) I was acquainted with a lot of the Crystal curlers, since I had gone to school with many of them. And I got to know a great bunch of people from Pilot Mound and community. When a new complex was built in Pilot Mound, the league moved to that location with three sheets of ice. This rink was built as a curling rink, and the ice was much superior. The Crystal rink had crooked ice, since winter frost affected the two outside sheets. When it was constructed, frost that would heave the floor hadn't been taken into consideration. I became a skip after the first few years, as well as adapting to throwing the rocks with a stick. Many of us old timers had difficulty getting down in the hack and sliding out to deliver the rock. The stick allowed one to walk out from the hack and release the rock before the hog line. Easier for those with back, hip, and leg issues, which affected most of us!

The league featured a regular schedule of two games a week, but there were also special daytime bonspiels in various towns within an hour's drive. We were requested to send a number of teams to these events, and then these clubs would send their teams our way when we held our local bonspiel. These were additional recreation/social events, as well as serving as fundraisers for the local clubs. Not all of our curlers wished to curl out of town. There was a core group that did want to go, and rinks were chosen from this group. I often went with one of these rinks.

Golfing was another sport I enjoyed. I had golfed since the late 1960s when my brother, Dave, gave me some instructions. It's a tough sport to learn! I golfed at every place we lived. One didn't need an opponent or a schedule. One just needed one other person to join. Golfing by oneself wasn't that enjoyable. It took on another dimension when I read about pasture golf in a magazine. It was a concept from the early days of golf in Scotland when golfing was done in sheep pastures! We now had the pasture as well as the sheep.

Duane and David pasture golfing, 2008

The terrain of our pasture would make an interesting course, so I designed one with nine "holes" at first and extended it with a few more eventually. There were no real holes. Instead, I used a five-gallon pail filled with sand and a flag stuck in it. The idea was to chip the ball when you reached the "green" and hit the pail instead of sinking the ball in a hole. That way, minimal mowing was required. The sheep trimmed up much of the pasture, and the occasional mowing of a circle around the pails created the size of a regular green. I had the time and interest to do this. The course was never very busy. Community people showed a lot of interest in the project, and I was often asked about it, but most preferred to golf on a regular course! It was a lot of fun for our family, however, as well as some of the B&B guests. Dave was home from Australia for a visit one summer. My course was in prime shape, and we played a round the first evening. After that first round, he accused me of designing it for my particular skill set. Several of the "holes" could be reached with an 8-iron, which was my most reliable club. My score was better than his, and he golfed regularly in Australia twice a week, all year round! Early the next morning, I looked out over the pasture from our upstairs bedroom, and there was Dave practising hitting the pail from different distances. I had perfected this stroke over the past while, and this had been his weakness. After that, our scores were more even!

The course might have been more popular if it hadn't been so difficult. It wasn't very suitable for youngsters to learn on. It crossed a ravine at three different places, and the creek on several more. It required a considerable amount of finesse not to continually lose your ball. So I guess it was built for me, and I sure enjoyed it for the years it was maintained. I'm somewhat embarrassed, but I do need to relate the following story. Our grandsons, Noah and Jem, were out for summer holidays the year I was getting the course established. We had finished putting the pails with the flags in place, and I suggested it was time to test the course. We gathered the necessary clubs and a good supply of balls and approached the first tee box. The first pail was across the ravine, so I took out the 8-iron! Just as I was about to hit the ball, the flock of sheep came through the trees and gathered around the pail. (These pails had been used to feed barley to the sheep in the winter, and they likely recognized them.) I decided to hit the ball anyway. The sheep had a coat of wool that would soften the blow if I happened to hit one. I launched a good looking shot and held my breath. The ball travelled across the ravine, bounced off the back of a sheep, and *ping*—hit the pail! Noah's jaw dropped, and he exclaimed, "Grandpa, you got a hole in one!" Well, technically, not a hole, rather a pail in one! The only one so far in my golfing career. It being the first shot on my pasture golf course made it memorable.

And having two eye-witnesses present was fortunate for me. Would people believe this story if only I had been there? This experience is not unlike my very first ewe giving birth to quadruplets back in 1962!

The first fall I helped my cousin with his harvest was in 1995. My labour that year was in exchange for the use of his truck and trailer to haul home the ewe lambs we had purchased in Saskatchewan. My skill in operating their combine must have passed inspection, so helping with their harvest became an annual event for the next fifteen years. We continued the swapping arrangement, with me using some of their equipment for haying and manure spreading. We were just completing the 2006 harvest on the farm that our fathers had occupied as teenagers when they came to Crystal City in 1928. I was contemplating some of these things and thought we, as Hildebrand descendants, should celebrate an anniversary of our family's arrival to Canada.

The one-hundred-year anniversary would be in 2028. By that time, many of us would be too old to plan such an event! An eighty-year anniversary would be more feasible. It could be held in 2008, which was two years away.

My mind was in a whirl. I had a team of horses and a wagon. We could re-trace the trek our family took in 1928 from the train station in Crystal City to the farm they had purchased five miles south of town, with the team leading the way. We could recount the stories from the past. Meanwhile, Judy and I had supper with my cousin and his family that evening. Harvest had been completed, and while eating dessert, I shared my musing. Art immediately declared that we should organize a reunion, so the idea was born. We decided to invite local cousins to a meeting and propose this plan to them. These cousins represented all but one of the six Hildebrand brothers (our fathers) who had farmed in the area between Crystal City and Mather.

The idea met with immediate approval, and all were excited to be involved in the planning. Proposed dates and a timeline for future planning meetings were set. I was asked to chair the committee. We had roughly eighteen months to plan for a full weekend of events for all age groups. We'd need to recruit a considerable amount of help from the younger generation, who had skills in areas where we were lacking. One of these tasks was to write a reader's theatre that would tell the story of the journey from

Life in Retirement

Southern Russia to the farm south of Crystal City. It was also suggested that a memorial cairn be built and unveiled the weekend of the reunion. A website was created that kept the larger family informed as the plans took shape. People were found for all these tasks! There was continuing anxiety as to how many people would respond and actually show up that weekend. Some thought that their children showed little interest. Others said theirs were fully committed! Planning continued with the idea of keeping costs to a minimum. There were a lot of meals to prepare, and catering at least one was discussed, but later the plan discarded. Alternative plans needed to be made in case of rain. The local hall, theatre, and campground were all reserved, and a large tent was erected in the park.

It turned out to be ideal weather for our event, and people came in droves, with registrations coming in up until the last week. The campground was full of tents and campers. There was enough food, and there were enough volunteers to assist with the meals and the cleanup. The highlight was the trek from town to the farm! The team of horses with the wagon loaded with kids led the way. People truly responded to retracing this last piece of the journey that our family had travelled eighty years ago. More than one hundred people participated by walking, biking, or riding on trailers.

Now we have the memories of this weekend, aided by a video and a booklet with pictures and the text of the reader's theatre. All the planning had been worth it. Capsules had been placed under the memorial cairn, with instructions that they be opened forty-five years later, in 2053! Hopefully, the younger generation will not forget to do this!

It was this same summer that we received new neighbours when the Patersons moved to the acreage just down the road. While they were younger than we were, we became truly good friends. We seemed to be of the same generation, and later, as they became grandparents, we boasted about our grandkids and compared how child-raising challenges had changed over the generations! When they moved back to Alberta in 2019, it took some adjusting for all of us.

During this retirement phase, life continued to be busy, even without a job to attend to. The B&B remained busy, the farm had year-round activity, and volunteer work and sports filled the weeks and months. Special times were when our family came for visits. We developed a pattern of hosting the family on the Thanksgiving weekend. Some of our kids hesitated to come for Christmas due to weather conditions, so the October event became an annual gathering when everyone was able to come. We didn't get to see Abby as much as the Manitoba grandkids, so it was great to see her with her cousins. There was an immediate rapport! There's something special about being cousins! (A little side story here: we had visited the Calgary Zoo with Abby when she was quite young. She was intrigued with the flamingos. Later, when we were back at their house, I'd ask her how the flamingos stand. She'd raise one of her legs and say, "One leg!") At Thanksgiving, the weather was usually good for the grandkids to play outside and explore the yard. The horses continued to be an attraction, as well as the trampoline. Julius was into skateboarding and always brought his skateboard along to the farm. We didn't have much space for this sport, but he'd drag a plywood sheet out of the garage, prop it up to make a slope, and practise his tricks! At night, of course, they all slept in the attic!

Winters provided other activities. I enjoyed the winters when the grandkids would come out to play under the bale shelter as I fed the sheep. Kathryn and Julius would often go out and play there on their own. On one occasion, a large group, including second cousins, was visiting. Kathryn slid down between the stacks of bales and almost disappeared. She needed some adult assistance to climb back up and escape her prison! She came back to the house with lots of alfalfa tangled in her hair. She had told the others not to tell Papa, for he might forbid them to play there in the future. What they actually created that day was folklore to talk about decades later!

Frieda and Johanna were born to Jason and Katharina during the last years we were on the farm, and they enjoyed farm experiences as well. Frieda made many trips out to the barn during winter lambing time. She would hold my hand as we trudged through the snow. I also recall placing her on the back of one of the horses, knowing it might be her last chance, as I was looking for a new home for my team. Unfortunately, they will have few memories of that stage of their life. Noah and Jem were teenagers and spent time outdoors on the snowmobile. They were now too old to play on the bales. The parents would cross-country ski and snowshoe along the creek. Some winters, skating could take place, and there were always sleigh rides during the holidays.

It had been twelve years since my retirement from pastoral work at Trinity, but we had continued our involvement in the congregation as "regular members." I was called upon to preach on occasion, which I accepted if the dates suited my busy schedule! Our pastor was granted a few months sabbatical after her first six years of service. Since she would be out of Canada for two months, I was asked to be on stand-by in case of emergency. I consented to this, not anticipating being called upon. Two members of our congregation were having health challenges but were expected, with treatment, to recover or at least stabilize. However, in both cases their health failed, and hospital visits needed to be made. Then both passed away within two months of each other. I assisted the bereaved families in funeral planning and then conducted the funerals. I knew the families well, and my service was appreciated, even though I confessed I was a bit "rusty." Our pastor came back home, somewhat dismayed with the two deaths. It was fortunate that arrangements had been made in case of emergency.

This first phase of my retirement was coming to an end. Plans were beginning to take shape for to the next phase. More decisions would need to be made!

Stage Two, 2015—2020

Life doesn't go on forever. One day we would need to leave our yard and the farm. Our kids realized this as well, as we occasionally talked about selling the farm. I was asked if there would be a part of the farmland that could be sub-divided for a yard site as a potential option for the future. I said there was no real good place. Some of the fields were prone to flooding, and others were too far from good road access or hydro connections. Then one day, I recognized a very natural site for a future yard on the home quarter section. It was a pie-shaped area of sixteen acres. A building site could be established overlooking the creek. It would be easy to subdivide, since the lane coming into the present yard would provide a natural boundary. I shared this idea with Judy, and she agreed it would be a good site for our kids to consider. When it came time to sell the yard and land, we would retain these sixteen acres.

One good idea is followed by another! Instead of reserving this site for our kids, why wouldn't we establish a yard there for ourselves and use it as our retirement place? And if we would follow this idea, we should do it sooner rather than later! We had planned on staying where we were for a number of years with the sheep and B&B, but if we waited too long, we might not have the energy to establish a new yard. Plans began to take shape. None of our family would be taking over the home place, so we'd look for a buyer for the yard and the home quarter-section, minus the acreage we would retain. When we informed our family of our thinking, one responded by asking if we really wanted to do all that work at our age. I said that I thought I would need to make about six phone calls to hire all the necessary labour. I'd call a surveyor, a contractor, hydro, well-driller, telephone, and one spare! We would just sit back and watch! It didn't end up that way, but we did get it done.

This was a major decision. Should we stay out in the country for the next years, or should we move into town, as most people retiring from the farm tended to do? Or should we relocate closer to Winnipeg? We were in the city for a visit while pondering this decision and decided to drive around the western part of Charleswood, wondering if we could live there. On our way home, we drove around Starbuck, checking out the old part of town as well as the new development. Neither of these options appealed to us, even though we knew the Starbuck community, since it was close to Springstein. We came home from that trip with our decision made. We would subdivide the site and establish a new yard! By the summer of 2015, this would be done, but much co-ordination would need to take place within the next year.

We needed to put our farm up for sale. I knew it might be difficult to sell. We had the large house and the barns with seventy acres of pasture along the creek and seventy acres of cropland. Would we find a buyer who would want this combination? We were planning on keeping our other 240 acres of cropland but would offer this land for rent if the buyer wanted it. We'd need to advertise this property by June 2014, but it the meantime, we let a few people know that the property would be up for sale.

One day in late winter, I noticed a car stopped on our lane. That wasn't completely unusual. It turned around and left after a while. A few weeks later, that same vehicle came into our yard, and a young man came to the house to say hello. He didn't indicate his reason for stopping by, but just as he was about to leave, Judy asked him if he knew our farm was for sale. He indicated he knew that but was very early in testing out this option. We invited him and his wife to come in and talk a bit about what might be possible. Their baby was sleeping in the car, but the sunshine was keeping her warm! They had a family of six children and were considering moving into our area if they found a suitable farm. Judy showed the mother the upstairs rooms and the attic, and she started deciding which of the children would use which of the rooms! It was very early in a long process, but by August 2015, the Friesens moved and began to make "our place" their home! They had already seeded the crop that spring on their new farm and on the rented land. They would make full use of every feature of what had been our place. A better match would have been hard to find!

Meanwhile, we had our own work to do! With the surveying completed for the sub-division, we made plans for the construction of our new home. We decided to create a "cabin feel." The building would be placed on the bank up from the creek and would have a walk-out basement. We would be able to cross-country ski or snowshoe right out of our basement! The main part of the cabin would have a vaulted ceiling with a knotty pine finish. We contracted KM Construction to build it for us. It would be moved from their construction site at Cartwright and was scheduled to arrive in June 2015. Timing would be critical, for August 1 was the occupancy date given to the Friesen family.

In early June, the house arrived. This was very exciting! By July 31, we had moved all our possessions into the upstairs of our new house, as well as filled the garage. We had spent our last night in the house we had moved into as a young married couple. We had lived there for seven years at the beginning of our marriage. We had left the farm and then returned twenty-two years later, just the two of us, to restore the house and make it our home for another twenty years. During those years, our adult children came to visit with spouses and youngsters in tow. We needed a break away from the place. Construction in our new basement would proceed in the next while. We left for a family gathering in Alberta, which would be followed by a houseboat holiday on a northern Saskatchewan lake with Rhonda, John, and family. Just two hours into our drive west, somewhere past Melita, a highway sign pointed south to Minot, North Dakota. I suggested we go south and retrace our honeymoon trip to the Black Hills that we had taken exactly fifty years earlier! But we'd miss our family gathering! Saner thoughts prevailed, and we said we'd go to the Black Hills the next summer, which we did.

While all these activities and planning for the next phase were taking place, I was recovering from a broken wrist. This had happened in March as I tangled with a ewe in the barnyard. This was the first broken bone I had suffered in my life! That same weekend, Raphael was born to Jason and Katharina. He was our ninth grandchild and completed that generation for us. I have a picture of me holding him with my blue cast visible!

While we were out west for ten days for our family gathering and houseboat adventure, work on our house proceeded. We had decided to hire Frank to install a three-season sunroom off our dining area, and this work progressed during our absence. This was a good addition to our cabin. Many meals take place in this space. Other work on the yard needed our attention the next year. We built retaining walls and a deck at the downstairs level for the walk-out. Dan, our neighbour, was the foreman for this project. We had created our own landscaping design and proceeded with establishing the lawn. We planted more trees around the yard, and I established what we now call "Papa's Little Forest." We had sixteen acres in total, so I used about one acre to plant several hundred trees! I chose Manitoba maples, poplars, several varieties of pine and spruce, as well as some lilacs and ornamental shrubs. I had some time to spare, so I nurtured these trees for several years. By keeping the ground tilled and weeded around each tree, growth happened more quickly. Young trees don't do well when competing with too much grass. I also needed to complete the barn with the loft and add the toboggan slide and the clothes line. My entire focus could be on the task at hand. There were no employment demands. There were no sheep to feed or any alfalfa to bale. There were no B&B guests! Only the garden and yard required our attention. Both of us were energized through this work. We weren't too old to take on this challenge! Retirement cannot be good without some direction and meaningful activity.

After our first year in our new place, and with these projects completed, life took on a routine established by the seasons. In spring and summer, we did quite a bit of gardening. There were lawns to mow and newly planted trees to till. In fall, we had potatoes to "lift" and corn to harvest. We often had a surplus, even after supplying our kids with their needs, and would deliver this produce to food banks. Since we had more time during this season, we started to take shorter four-day trips to parts of Manitoba we weren't familiar with. We had never been to the southeast Vita and Piney area, which included the northwest angle of Minnesota. Due to a surveying mistake a few centuries ago, this part of the USA is north of the Canadian border! We also toured the Winnipeg River area and the beaches of Lake Winnipeg, and another year we went to the inter-lake region. There were several travel guides available that featured out-of-the-way attractions. One summer we traced our way along Campbell Beach from the USA border to the Riding Mountains. This is a beach of the ancient Lake Agassi that was formed with the melting of the Ice Age. I believe very few Manitobans are familiar with this astonishing part of our geography. I discovered it featured in Bill Redekop's book, *Lake Agassiz, the Rise and Demise of the World's Greatest Lake*. Bill provides all the necessary directions needed to travel along this beach. Road signs don't indicate the route!

One fall, we decided to tour northern Manitoba instead of taking an out-of-province trip. I had been at The Pas in 1962 but had never been to Flin Flon or Thompson. Since we would be travelling through Swan River, I contacted my roommate from U of M days. We shared birthdays and had regular phone calls on this date for the past several years. However, his daughter informed me that Jim was in the hospital and not expected to be home for a while. I told her that we would stop at the hospital and see him there. When we arrived three days later, we checked into our hotel and then found our way to the hospital. It was early evening, and the reception area was closed, but a nurse told me there was no patient by the name we gave her. She couldn't tell us if he had been a patient or where he might be now. We asked if he had been transferred to the nearby nursing home. She didn't say she didn't know; she just insisted she couldn't tell us. This was due to privacy legislation that had come into effect a few years earlier. I was aware of it, since I'd been on the hospital board at that time. I felt sorry for her. I could see that it pained her to turn us away. Later, we made a phone call to Jim's home. His daughter informed us that her dad had passed away the day after I had called. We had missed saying goodbye by one day. (On the topic of privacy legislation, a few years later, Judy had gone to our local hospital on her daily visit to her mom, who was a patient. After she left for town, I called the hospital and asked for an appointment for a minor ailment. When I approached the nursing desk, Judy was talking to the nurses about her mother's medication and didn't notice me coming in. When she noticed me, she asked me what I was doing there. I replied, "Due to privacy legislation, I am unable to tell you!" The nurses and the doctor behind the desk burst out laughing!)

We were still enjoying annual fall trips, and there were still places we hoped to tour. Newfoundland was one of them, and what an excellent experience that turned out to be. We journeyed there by plane and then toured most of the province with a rented car. The people are exceedingly friendly. One day late in the afternoon, we were looking for a specific museum in a small town. There was a group of boys, eleven to thirteen years of age, along the road, so we asked them for directions. We had driven by the museum, having missed the sign. But these boys wanted to visit when they found out we were from the prairies. When we told them we lived on a farm, one asked if we had pigs! More questions were forthcoming, and then they asked us what we liked about their province. We shared a few highlights and then we told him we liked the ocean and all the bays. The waves coming into shore were fascinating. One of the boys responded, clearly not impressed, with, "Oh, the water, it's always there!"

Another trip happened quite unexpectedly. Four curlers, myself being one of them, had entered a +55 Manitoba curling bonspiel. We ended up winning the event, and before being awarded the gold medals, were informed that we qualified to go to the +55 Canada Games that would be held in St. John, New Brunswick in August! But we didn't have much time to decide. Over beer and Sprite (me), we considered the possibility and concluded we really wanted to go! In August we were on the ice at St. John. Elfrieda joined Judy and me for this trip. We had two cheerleaders from our family, and the other three curlers brought four more. Our group of three flew into Quebec City, rented a car, and spent several days touring the St. Lawrence River, south shore, and then into New Brunswick. We hadn't covered much of this area earlier. The time in St. John was fantastic.

We didn't win any of the four games, but we were competitive in each one! A few years later, I asked one of the curlers on our rink what he considered the highlight of his many decades of curling to be, and he didn't hesitate. He said it was the experience at the Canada Games! (We were entered in the +65 category, but two us qualified for +75!)

Our children had decided to buy their mom a bike for her seventieth birthday. They thought that she would use it. Then they decided to buy one for me as well, thinking we might bike together. Well, we have done just that. We purchased a bike rack to attach to our car and have taken the bikes on most of our car trips since then. We've biked in more than forty locations in the four western provinces as well as in Ontario, and in five states of the USA! Two of our favourite biking locations are Swift Current, Saskatchewan and Camrose, Alberta. We've biked these several times. Our last major car trip was through Ontario, where we biked at seven different locations. A favourite one on that trip was at Orangeville, where we biked on a great nature trail around a small lake. Biking was almost as much fun as watching the Blue Jays baseball game and the Saskatchewan Roughrider game, both being played in Toronto on the same weekend!

Judy and Ernie on Judy's seventieth birthday, 2014

While we enjoyed travelling, living on our acreage was enjoyable as well. We had carved out a campfire spot closer to the creek in a wooded area. This grove featured a big, old maple tree! I'd estimate by the size of the trunk that the tree could be over two hundred years old. This became a great place for wiener roasts. I had mowed this area the fall before we established the yard. It had been pasture for cattle, but we built a fence around it to keep the cattle out. When the family came that fall on the Thanksgiving weekend, our plan was to host the family there for the noon wiener roast. It was a warm but windy day. We hardly felt the wind in this sheltered spot. I meant this event to be an introduction to our new yard. The family agreed that it was a great feature. The younger ones explored the creek and climbed the old maple tree. We adults spent a few hours sitting on lawn chairs and just enjoying each other with fall nature all around us. Before returning to our old yard, they wanted to know exactly where we intended to place our proposed cabin. I had placed some stakes where I thought it could be placed. It was agreed that the place had potential.

We have now had several years of living on this place and sharing it with our family. The youngest three grandkids hadn't experienced the farmyard like the older ones. Their memories will be formed on this new yard. They all enjoy the outdoors in all seasons. It's a great place to fly their kites. In the wide-open space, there's usually enough wind. Frieda built extensive tunnels in the snowbanks in the winter, spending hours outside even under very cold conditions. Johanna also enjoys the outdoors. Jumping on the trampoline is a favourite activity. She also spends a lot of time indoors. She might be the one to become our family's accomplished author! At an early age, she's already writing lengthy fiction stories. She staples the pages together and leaves them for us to read when they leave for their home in the city. We read them and try to puzzle out the plot! She also created elaborate restaurant settings with printed menus featuring her favourite items. Prices were listed for each item! Raphael loved exploring outside. When he was four years old, he discovered a ravine where he loved to spend his time. It was some distance from our yard, and he needed adult accompaniment to go there. He would need to cross the creek twice, but he knew the way. One day, he recruited three different adults at three different times to make the trek with him, and he tried to convince them to stay there with him for more than an hour at a time.

Michelle had asked me when we decided on this second stage of retirement if I worried about becoming depressed as my activity decreased. I told her if we were moving into a third-floor apartment in Winnipeg, I would fear that I might. But not if I stayed in the country, especially the setting we had chosen!

I just stepped outside on our lower deck. It's just outside of my den, where I've been writing these stories for the last four months. It's mid-March. The snow is mostly gone. The weather is unseasonably warm. A blue jay flies, cawing for it's mate, into the bush. A few Canada geese were spotted last week. The trampoline awaits the arrival of the grandkids. A great-grandson, Kaiden, was born a year ago to Noah and Breanne. Maybe he'll come for a visit this summer. The start of a new generation. The large maple tree is bare, but leaves will eventually emerge. It is showing its age, just like Judy and me!

Family at Judy and Ernie's Fiftieth Wedding Anniversary, 2015

Afterword

I recall being at a local ministerial meeting with fellow clergy from United, Anglican, and Mennonite congregations. I was telling them about a book I had read in which the author cautioned pastors not to refer to some of their parishioners as jerks. He said a lot of people in the church are chronically anxious. One of the ministers at the meeting burst out laughing and said, "That describes me perfectly. I'm chronically anxious!" There you have it! It really doesn't matter if you're clergy or laity, religious or secular, we're still all people with similar ailments we need to cope with. People in the church are expected to be "better" than people claiming no religious affiliation. Yet Jesus spoke about his coming for those who are sick. Those who are well have no need of a physician.

I've spent my lifetime in the church, much of it in leadership. Even though I retired from pastoral work eighteen years ago, I was reminded recently that I'm still seen as a pastor. I was golfing and sharing a cart with a good friend. One member of our foursome was a guest, and partway through the round, he was told I was a pastor. I told him I was very, very retired! Back on the cart, I told my friend that I was puzzled that I was still seen as a pastor after all these years. He said I would always be seen as one!

Yet all my life, I have also lived in the "secular" world. Many people that one associates with are not part of the "religious" world. I have seen the good and the not-so-good in both worlds. While pastors often tend to point out the good in the church and the bad in the "world," I'll provide just a few examples of good experiences in the "world."

For several years, Judy and I played slow-pitch baseball at Swift Current, in what was known as a "beer" league. We had a great time. While our team members were mostly connected with the Bible school, the other teams were sponsored by an assortment of businesses from the city. Later, I played in a church league based in Winnipeg. Teams came from as assortment of Evangelical churches. The competition was fierce. It seemed every team had to prove that their church was superior. I longed to play again in a beer league!

Judy had a variety of customers in her consignment store at Swift Current. One evening she told me about one visit that afternoon. A young mother was shopping. She came from a farm an hour south of the city. There was no one else in the store, so she told a bit about herself. She had been part of a motorcycle gang when she was young. The gang was into drinking and drugs. One day, she decided to leave that life. She married a farmer and now was raising her children on the farm. She made no mention of it being a religious experience. As Judy related her story, I suggested that one could see it as a secular conversion!

I delivered some sheep and lambs to a ranch north of Winnipeg. The contact person was a Muslim acquaintance of ours who had spent time at our B&B. The delivery was for the annual Muslim celebration when they butcher many animals and share one third of the food with a community in need. While waiting for the arrival of my contact, the rancher offered to show me his set-up. I got into his half-ton with him, and we began to tour his farm. He soon opened the window of the truck a bit and lit his cigarette. After a while, I commented that I didn't think that Muslims smoked. He said that he wasn't a very good Muslim. I admired him for his honesty. I told him that there were also a lot of Christians who could say that they weren't very good Christians! Yet, like him, they were engaged in doing good deeds!

As a person of faith, I view the above examples as glimpses of "God" at work. I chose to share these three examples, for they could be considered coming from rather unexpected places. These glimpses can be seen, however, all over in religious and non-religious settings. They're not restricted to the church as we have often been led to believe.

Afterword

For me, it's not going to church that's of utmost importance. It's belonging to a community of faith. It's joining with others and being able to discuss the "big" issues of life and death. It's being with people you can trust to stick with you, even though you do some stupid things and believe some things that may puzzle them. A place where you're given the benefit of the doubt. This community is not restricted to a specific congregation. One finds "kindred" spirits all over!

I have always been curious and often wished more people would be curious as well.

I believe that all of life is sacred. It takes some time to come to that realization!

I'd like to acknowledge the major contribution that Judy has made to the writing of this book. The story is mine, but the first drafts I wrote weren't always coherent. She knew what I was wanting to say and re-arranged my sentences so that the reader could better understand. She has been supportive throughout this venture and never suggested deleting any stories I had chosen to include. Also thanks to our four children, who reviewed some of the chapters and offered total support. I have also relied on them for technical assistance and advice in transferring documents, and pictures onto the computer. I chose Friesen Press to bring this story to print. They have been a true pleasure to work with! Thank-you.

Tribute to Linda

Linda Marie Hildebrand was born on March 24, 1947, to Jake and Margaret Hildebrand. I do remember the trip home with new little sister, Linda. The road west from the highway to our farm was a muddy dirt road, and it had rained. We drove partway in the ditch to get around particularly bad sections of road! Linda moved into the little house with the four of us. An addition (eight-by-fourteen) had been added to the original building (fourteen-by-sixteen) when Elfrieda was born. I heard it said that Linda soon demanded better living conditions, so Dad started building a new house that spring! By fall it was ready, and we all enjoyed the spacious one-and-a-half-storey house, wired to ready it for hydro in a few years. Lucky for David who joined the family a year later!

I remember Linda as a happy child. Elfrieda was my companion, and Linda was the kid sister. She shared a room with Elfrieda and had her own activities. She enjoyed school, made good friends, and was loved in the family. We older ones had chores to do, but she played. We didn't mind. One summer she spent a few holidays with Aunt Elsie. Her aunt had commented on how good a helper she was and how Mom must be proud of her. Linda had replied, "Oh no, I don't work at home. If I would start, I would need to work every day."

Life changed abruptly when she was just nine years old. She was diagnosed with bone cancer, and her leg was amputated at her hip to save her life. After agonizing pain lasting several months, healing took place. She became very adept with crutches and could keep up with everyone. She had understood that she would be fitted with an artificial limb after the surgery and had been disappointed when that wasn't the case right after her operation. But a limb was eventually fitted and the adjustment of walking with it began.

For the next years, she managed well and was generally upbeat. She could participate in most of the activities of early teenage years. Then another major blow hit our family. Mom had suspected failing health, and after visits to the doctor, it was confirmed that cancer had re-occurred. She was fifteen years old. She declined rapidly, and death was imminent. We gathered as a family in the General Hospital in Winnipeg. Grandma Harms was also with us. It was to be Linda's last day with us. She had woken that morning having had a dream that she was in heaven, and she was disappointed that she was still alive. She proceeded to instruct all of us to sip from a cup of water that she passed around. Grandma said that she wasn't thirsty. She was told it was "Abendmahl" (the Lord's supper), so she also took a sip. An amazing act for one who had not yet experienced this ceremony in church. Later, she gave Mom instructions on how to dispose of her possessions. A favourite bathrobe was to be sent to a girl she had met at a camp for crippled children at Gimli. (That's what the camp was called in the 1960s.) She faced death with great courage, which made it a little bit easier for all of us. She died on Tuesday, June 5, 1962. I realize now that grieving for a mother who loses her child lasts all her life.

The funeral was held in the home church on Saturday, June 9, 1962. She is buried in the Crystal City cemetery, where her parents are now also buried, one on each side. Hers was the first death in the larger Harms family. Rest in peace.

Submitted by Ernie Hildebrand (2018)

Guatemalan Guest is now Springstein's "Disappeared"

by Barbara Shewchuk

There's a spot on the front pew in the Springstein Mennonite Church where Pastor Ernie Hildebrand's eyes are bound to stray during this year's Christmas Day service.

Last Christmas, William sat there.

No one knows where William is today, or if he is dead or alive. He disappeared on January 3, leaving no details about his plans, only a note saying, "Ernie, I had to leave. I am going back home."

William Lopez came into the lives of Ernie Hildebrand, his family and his congregation in May, 1991, when church member Bill Enns saw him hitchhiking west along Wilkes Blvd. in Winnipeg. Mr. Enns didn't usually pick up hitchhikers, but the boy looked "tired, hungry and innocent," said Mr. Hildebrand.

In Springstein, the Ennses fed William and then, unsure what-to-do with him, called their pastor.

The story that unfolded from the 15-year-old Guatemalan then and over the next few weeks seemed almost fantastic, but the details William related convinced even Canadian Immigration officials he was telling the truth.

Raised by an abusive, often absentee father who seemed to have connections with both the Guatemalan military and anti-government guerrillas, William had never known his mother or siblings. His father's beatings were so bad William had ended up in hospital, Mr. Hildebrand said. The last straw was his father's pressure to have him join the military.

"I didn't want to kill," William told his new friends in Canada. So he fled from his remote village near the El Salvador border riding freight trains across Mexico, using a found Mexican passport to enter the United States, hopping more freights to California, up the west coast to Washington, and all the way east to Boston.

There he met some legal immigrants from Nicaragua who advised him to go to Canada and accompanied him by bus to the Midwest. William crossed the border at the International Peace Garden without any problems—much to the chagrin of the Canadian Immigration officials who were later told about it, Mr. Hildebrand said. He bused it to Winnipeg, spent the night under a bridge, and followed train tracks, intending to hop a freight train to Montreal. But he ended up heading west on Wilkes.

After consulting with interfaith immigration and Mennonite Central Committee representatives, William decided to "take his chances" with Canadian Immigration. To everyone's relief, Immigration, instead of jailing William, appointed the Hildebrands his guardian.

"You Mennonite people get all the breaks," quipped the Roman Catholic priest who served as a translator.

Living in a room vacated by one of the Hildebrand's adult children, William spent the tail-end of the school year at Starbuck School, then revelled in a carefree summer of long bike rides on the 10-speed he was given. He cycled as far as Winnipeg Beach and once biked all the way home from Clear Lake.

"He liked to explore—he prided himself on his stamina and his muscular build," said Mr. Hildebrand. In fall, backed by a support group from the Springstein church, he enrolled in West- gate Mennonite Collegiate in Winnipeg, which has an English as a Second Language (ESL) program. "He wanted to get an education and to travel," Mr. Hildebrand continued; "he wanted to become a pilot, or even a truckdriver, just to travel."

But with the onset of winter, William became restless. He had never been regulated much, he had worked and roamed freely with his friends in Guatemala. Added to the routine of school was the snow, which interfered with his cycling, and the (to him) cold. "By December, he threatened to leave—in a storm," Mr. Hildebrand said. "We talked him out of it."

Counselling seemed to help William; he became jovial and lighthearted, but in retrospect the Hildebrands believe William had already made up his mind to leave.

"Winter is almost over," he told the Hildebrands at Christmastime. "No, it is only half over," Mr. Hildebrand insisted. "William kept insisting winter was over. Maybe he meant, 'winter is over for me.'"

Christmas was a happy time for William. Although he hated winter, he loved snowmobiling with Judy Hildebrand's family at Crystal City. Family gatherings were new to him. "I don't know my grandparents. Why?" he would ask.

On Christmas Day, 1991, William Lopez sat in the front pew at the Springstein Mennonite Church. He had always come to church with the Hildebrands, but had always sat near the back and "kind of roamed around" during services. Ernie Hildebrand, looking down from the pulpit, was surprised. And then he was amazed.

William turned around to the hymn presenters who sat in the pew behind him and asked Bill Enns, the man who had picked him up on the road, if he could present a selection.

"Here we have a 16-year-old Guatemalan boy serving as a presenter ... very unique," Mr. Hildebrand recalled. "He had the boldness to choose."

Was the hymn, Number 475, a message to the congregation, or just "a fluke?" wonders Mr. Hildebrand.

> "Father, we thank Thee for the night
> and for the pleasant morning light
> For rest and food and loving care
> and all that makes the day so fair.
> Help us to do the things we should
> to be to others, kind and good
> In all we do at work and play
> to grow more loving every day."

"That was a startling thing."

More startling still was William's disappearance during January 3, and yet, in retrospect, clues were there. William took his bicycle and rode away from Springstein, leaving only a brief note. The RCMP, alerted by the Hildebrands, did not actively search for him but kept his file on record in case a missing person, or, worse, a frozen body should be found.

But William has never been found. "We had a Third World experience in our own congregation," Mr. Hildebrand said. The Springstein community glimpsed the fear and hardship pervasive in other countries. "Now we have a missing person, just like all those people with 'Disappeared' loved ones (in repressive countries) and the Mennonites who were in Europe through the Russian Revolution and World War periods. It's really kind of sobering."

"'What happened to William?'" People ask. People care. "He was here long enough to make quite an impression." Did he return to Guatemala, or head west to British Columbia? Is he alive?

Ernie Hildebrand and the members of his congregation may never know. But they'll always remember the boy who lived in their midst, and who presented a song on Christmas Day.

"You have to put it out of your hands," concluded Mr. Hildebrand, "and let it rest in the hands of God and the lucky powers that helped him get this far."

From *Crow King Warrior,* Christmas Edition, Morris, Manitoba. December 1992.

A January Morning on the Farm

It is January and snowing again! The road to the highway is blocked after the last two days of drifting snow. It might be possible to get out with the four-wheel drive, but even that isn't guaranteed. We'll wait for the snowplow to come.

Meanwhile, life is not boring! There's a lot of activity, work, excitement, and joy here on the farm! It's lambing time! To make the trek across the yard, trudging through drifts while breathing in the icy air that makes you cough, and then to open the door to the warm barn with all its new life is exhilarating! Visualize twelve pens, each four feet by five feet in size, and each being home to a new mama with her one or two or three or four newborn lambs! Some lambs are warming up under heat lamps, but most of them are well on their way and having sufficient body heat of their own. Everything is quiet—everyone is content! Slowly the mamas get up after the light is turned on. The lambs stretch and eagerly nose around for their first drink of the morning.

The shepherd was out at the barn at 4:00 a.m. and brought a mama and a new set of twins in at that time. The twins are a good size and have full tummies, meaning the mama has lots of milk. Now, at 8:00 a.m., the shepherd checks the colder, loose-housing west wing of the barn, but there are no lambs to be seen or heard.

Each mama in her little pen needs to be fed her pan of barley, given a drink of water, and fed a wad of hay. This task—and to cuddle a few lambs—is the job of the shepherd's helper. In the meantime, the shepherd goes to do the outside chores, feeding hay to the pregnant ewes in the corral.

When chores are done and it's time to return to the house, the pregnant ewes need to be checked one more time. One ewe has stayed in the barn instead of going out to eat. She already has two newborn lambs next to her! One lamb is on its feet; the second one struggling in the straw, trying to stand up on its weak legs, and being licked off by Mama. We watch for a while—the miracle of birth! By her pawing and turning around before she lies down, we can tell the mama will birth another lamb. As we watch, she begins to push, and almost immediately a head appears. Another push and the lamb, still in its birth sac, plops out! The shepherd pulls the new lamb around in front of the ewe, who, though she is tired, starts to lick off this lamb as well, beginning with the mouth and nose. The lamb shakes its head a few times, coughs, and begins to breathe. As mama continues to lick, the lamb lifts its head, eager to greet the world!

The days are busy with the shepherd making the trip to the barn to check for new lambs, sometimes aid a difficult birth, and water the ewes at least seven times in twenty-four hours. But to experience all this new life in the dead of winter makes farm life purposeful and enjoyable.

Judy Hildebrand

November 11, 2016
PM Justin Trudeau
House of Common
Ottawa, ON
K1A 0A6

Dear Prime Minister,

This is the first time I have written to a Prime Minister. I'm not too sure if you will actually read this letter, or if a staff member will read it and pass the message on to you, or if I will simply receive a message back thanking me for my concern while disregarding the content. I hope you get to read it or at least be informed as to the content.

I want to congratulate you on your election win and the first year of governing. While there may not be many Liberal supporters in rural western Canada, there are at least a small number here impressed with "a breath of fresh air!" I am personally impressed with the youthful energy you bring to the position.

My concern and suggestion. I read Ernie Regehr's book, *Disarming Conflict*, this past year. Regehr has spent a lifetime with Project Ploughshares working to advance policies and actions to prevent war and build peace. See www.projectplougshares.ca . In his latest book, he examines in great detail how wars of the past 4–5 decades have started and how they finally end. His conclusion is that in the majority of cases, armed conflict does not resolve the conflict. Negotiation is required to settle the issues when the two sides get tired of fighting. So why not start with negotiation when there is a conflict within a country, or between countries that will likely lead to war. This is an extremely brief summary of a very detailed book.

I ask you, as a Canadian Prime Minister, and as a world leader, to read this book or get a staff member to read it and provide you with a more detailed summary. Then, if you are persuaded with the message, place it on the agenda of the next G20 and G7 meetings. I have faith in your standing among other world leaders. I want to believe you would be listened to. The world has to find a way to resolve conflicts and prevent wars. Whenever there is a war, there is almost immediately a shortage of food, water, shelter, health care, education, etc. There never seems to be a shortage of bullets or bombs. And when the war ends, there are never enough resources to rebuild the damage done.

I'm a simple sheep farmer (now retired), but here is my suggestion.

—from the $1,000,000,000,000(over 1 trillion) + world military budget, keep 1/4 for the military for the time being for search & rescue and backing up negotiations.

—allocate 1/4 to training teams of negotiators and converting arms manufacturers from designing and building weapons of destruction to products that enhance life. I'm sure the cost of one fighter jet would train many people in negotiation skills. The U of Winnipeg would be a likely spot for such training. So the bulk of this budget would be for converting the present factories of arms of which Canada has a far number.

—the remaining 1/2 of the one trillion could be spent on making this earth a more equitable place. In Canada, finally providing First Nations peoples with water, housing, education, and health services, for example. We would have over $5,000,000,000 out of our military budget for that.

This plan may have many flaws, but I present it as a way to solve many problems we face at the still beginning of this century. Keep in mind, that there is no additional spending required. Simply a diverting of funds. And it is an annual diverting. "beating swords into ploughshares."

Thank you for reading. I trust you will get a second term to implement this plan if I have indeed convinced you!!

    Sincerely,
    Ernest J. Hildebrand
    Box 443
    Crystal City, MB
    R0K 0N0

Hildebrand Reunion 2008

The beautiful weekend of July 25–27 treated our family royally as we gathered in Crystal City to commemorate the eightieth anniversary of our family's coming to this community. Not a complaint was heard about the weather, mosquitos, facilities (or the relatives!) as 210 family members gathered from as far away as Qatar, Australia, California, Illinois, Ontario, and British Columbia.

Friday evening commenced with a wiener roast in the park. We then gathered in the Parklane Theatre, where a thirteen-member cast, dressed in period costume, performed the first part of the reader's theatre. The family's story was traced from 1789, when a Peter Hildebrand left East Prussia to emigrate to the Ukraine with the promise of land and freedom. The story centered on the 1920s and the difficult decision to again pull up roots and move to Canada. War, revolution, famine, disease, death, and the uncertainty of the future had resulted in over twenty thousand Mennonite people leaving the Ukraine for Canada. Our family decided to apply for the necessary papers and also make this move. There was much to ponder after these presentations.

After a pancake breakfast in the Community Hall on Saturday morning, we all gathered at the site of the former CPR station. The sound of the whistle of a steam engine alerted the gathering. The cast of the reader's theatre was seen approaching us as the sounds of long ago— the huffing, puffing, hissing—grew louder and louder. The cast mounted the stage and continued their story, telling of their long journey and their stay in Winnipeg over the winter of 1927–28. Now they had arrived at Crystal City on April 12, 1928. After hearing their story, we assembled at the park, preparing to re-trace the journey our family had taken eighty years earlier to Willow Brook Farm, five-and-a-half miles southwest of town. Trek marshals prepared the huge crowd. With a team of horses and wagon, loaded with children leading the way, the trek commenced. Three trailers with straw bales loaded with people followed. Others rode bikes. One rode a unicycle the whole distance. Two took turns on horseback. Then there were the walkers. While some chose to ride in vehicles, many more decided to walk, either the whole distance or a good portion of the distance. Our oldest cousin, Elizabeth, at seventy-nine years of age, walked the entire trek! People seemed determined to retrace this journey like a pilgrimage. It was an opportunity to relive a part of our ancestors' life, and at the same time connect with the descendants who were now sharing the journey. The trek took two hours to complete and at times stretched close to a mile in length.

A picnic lunch awaited us when we arrived at the farm, now owned by Carol Gardiner. The setting was beautiful and the weather just right for the picnic enjoyed under the shade of the trees that would have been there eighty years before. More stories were told about life at the farm, and then we moved to the southwest corner of 2-2-12 to unveil a memorial sign. This sign is a permanent tribute to the family that came in 1928

The trip back to town went more quickly, as we opted for vehicle transportation. People were now free to do as they chose. Some relaxed in the park; others toured the cemetery and the memorial garden. The historical displays in the hall received a lot of attention. Children enjoyed the activities planned for them and rode on the horse glider swing in the park that their grandparents had played on sixty years ago. After a delicious roast beef supper in the hall, we assembled in the park for a variety night with numerous stories and songs. Fireworks concluded a very full day. Not all had the stamina to stay till the end!

Afterword

Sunday began with a worship service under the big tent in the park. We sang familiar hymns, read scripture, and heard sermons contemplating life, faith, and journey. A brunch in the hall concluded the event. The gathering was appreciated by all and was truly a once in a lifetime experience!

Submitted by Ernie Hildebrand

+55 Canada Games

Curling in August. On the East Coast. Walking into the rink in shorts with mid-twenties temperature outside and changing to long johns and long pants! We experienced this and so much more in St. John, New Brunswick, August 20–24, 2018 at the 55+ Canada Games.

Before we left, we talked about our anticipations. Meet lots of people, have a fun time, win some games, be competitive, were some of the responses. We achieved three out of four. We didn't win any games, but not for lack of effort. It was like regular curling at home, just on a bigger stage with more hype. A hogged rock, a missed last shot, a sweeping error, an opponent's lucky shot (missed the broom then wicked off a guard to take out our shot hidden in the four foot), missed guard, a heavy draw. These are all features of curling at many levels. Just one of these shots can determine a win or loss.

We had a practice hour at 10:00 p.m. on Monday and then curled our first game at 9:00 a.m. on Tuesday. Tied after four ends, we gave up four on the fifth, which made it difficult to stage a comeback. The second game went eight ends with the Saskatchewan skip making a great draw behind cover, which we were not able to remove. That game ended close to midnight! The next two games on Wednesday also went to the last rocks in the eighth end. (So we were competitive.)

What was the competition like? We were led to believe they would be regular senior club rinks. Not so! The local New Brunswick rink had a skip whose family has Canadian Junior and Brier experience. His second had been on a rink that won the Canadian Seniors in 2014 and had gone on to Scotland to win there with a 12–0 record. We curled them in their home club and were tied after four ends! The Ontario skip said he had curled against Ed Wernick and Russ Howard in provincials but wasn't able to win against them. We lost to them by missing our last shot! We played tough against all three medal winners.

We didn't leave there hanging our heads. (A lot of other games had lopsided scores.) It would have been nice to win a game or two, but maybe next time!

St. John is a beautiful city with many old buildings, lovely parks, and an amazing natural setting on the mouth of the St. John River. The Bay of Fundy tides cause this river to reverse its flow twice a day, therefore billed as the "Reversing Falls." The crowd at the curling rink from across Canada were friendly and very talkative. Seniors are active people and curling well into their eighties. Besides the curling, a great part of the games was all the social interaction with everyone there, not just the curlers, but any of the other participants and spectators that were there. A fellow from Saskatchewan told me his wife was curling in the 65+ game. He said, "We've been married for forty-three years, and my wife says twelve good ones!" What a sense of humour!

There were three other Manitoba curling teams in St. John: 65+ women from Glenboro, 55+ women from Manitou (won bronze), and 55+ men from Dauphin (won silver).

Thanks for all your interest, and we appreciated the six loyal fans we had there cheering us on.

Submitted by Ernie Hildebrand for Bob Boyd, Neil Windsor, & Morley Johanson.

Printed in Canada